CW00642286

Terriers for Sport

by

Pierce O'Conor

Read Country Books
Home Farm
44 Evesham Road
Cookhill, Alcester
Warwickshire
B49 5LJ

www.readcountrybooks.com

ISBN No. 1-905124-31-7

Published by Read Country Books 2005

British Library Cataloguing-in-Publication Data
A catalogue record for this book is available
from the British Library.

Read Country Books
Home Farm
44 Evesham Road
Cookhill, Alcester
Warwickshire
B49 5LJ

CAPT. JOCELYN LUCAS AND MR. A. A. SIDNEY VILLAR WITH A TEAM
OF SEALYHAM TERRIERS AFTER DIGGING OUT A 35LB.
BADGER.

TERRIERS FOR SPORT.

By
PIERCE O'CONOR.

PUBLISHED BY
"OUR DOGS" PUBLISHING CO. LTD.,
"OUR DOGS" BUILDINGS,
OXFORD ROAD STATION APPROACH,
MANCHESTER.

CONTENTS.

Index to Illustrations.

CAPT. JOCELYN LUCAS "TAILING" THE BADGER.

TERRIERS FOR SPORT.

BY PIERCE O'CONOR.

INTRODUCTORY.

In offering these few notes to my readers I do so not with any idea of instructing men who have hunted Terriers themselves, for they may well know more about the game than I do. My aim is rather to provide the uninitiated with a brief outline of the various sports that may be enjoyed with a small Terrier pack, and to give them a few general hints on working and caring for their dogs.

The notes were primarily prepared for the use and benefit of poor men, men who, though they cannot afford the now costly pleasures of fox-hunting, shooting, etc., are still imbued with a love of the chase and a life in the open.

Terrier sport, however, is by no means necessarily confined to the uses of the indigent. People with ample means at their disposal can also get a great deal of fun and amusement out of a Terrier pack, one of its greatest charms being the absence of any need for elaborate preparation for the hunt. You just whistle your little pack and off you go, wherever and whenever your fancy takes you.

There are many people, of course, in these times who for lack of cash or the necessary outhouse accommodation, or a variety of other reasons, cannot keep more than one or two Terriers. For such the best plan is to get hold of three or four others similarly placed, and to form a club. This is quite a workable arrangement, and has much to recommend it ; indeed, for badger digging it is to be preferred to individual effort, as the cost, which might be too high for one man to bear, becomes very moderate when divided amongst many ;

also the good fellowship and friendly rivalry which a club engenders in the matter of dogs and kennels are all to the good.

Where otter or stoat hunting is concerned, the " trencher-fed " system no doubt has its drawbacks. It will be well-nigh impossible to get the dogs to acknowledge one master, and fights will be of frequent occurrence.

These little matters, however, are but difficulties to be overcome or made the best of. The great thing is to get two or three couple of dogs together and go ahunting, and then you will learn something every day.

It may not be out of place here to warn such of my readers as have not had much experience in these matters that no hunting of any kind should be undertaken without first obtaining the permission of the owners or occupiers of the land, and that every care should be taken to avoid disturbing game or farm stock, or causing any damage to property.

Finally, I would suggest that in any district your activities should commence with ratting, and if, after a while, you can show a goodly toll of slain, farmers and others are more apt to believe in your *bona fides*, and exhibit a friendly spirit towards the " hunt."

Gamekeepers should always be treated with the greatest deference and consideration. They can be your best friends or your worst enemies.

It need hardly be said that wild dogs, or those addicted to chasing sheep or killing poultry, cannot be tolerated at any price, and if in the field any dog shows the least unsteadiness in this respect he must be coupled up or put in a leash till all danger of temptation is passed.

Always replace turf and earth displaced by digging, and never forget to close all gates behind you.

GETTING A TEAM TOGETHER.

Although the choice of a breed for a working pack may be left to individual fancy and length of purse, there can be no question as to the qualities essential in a working Terrier—viz., pluck, hardiness, and nose, and all in a sufficiently small compass to enable him to go to ground and work there ; for be it known there are many heavy oversized dogs that will go into an earth eagerly enough, but once there cannot get up to their quarry and stay with him, a most necessary consideration in badger digging.

There are a great variety of Terriers on the market in these days, but for our purpose we may ignore all save the Fox, the Sealyham, and the Border Terrier. There may be, and no doubt are, good ones amongst the others, but they are not regularly bred for sporting purposes, and so are outside our province.

Of the three breeds mentioned the Fox is the oldest, and for long had a virtual monopoly of the hunting business, but in the last few years the Sealyham has become increasingly popular with sporting men, and in the North of England the Border Terrier has had a great boom in spite of a somewhat mean and uncomely appearance. There is probably nothing much to choose between the three breeds in the matter of hunting qualities. The great demand for Sealyhams and Borders, however, has run their price up to such fancy figures as to put them rather outside the means of any but the wealthy.

Having settled the question of the breed you fancy, you will probably wish to obtain two or more adult dogs already entered to sport as a nucleus for your pack, and so you can get on with the work. If you can get these locally from animals well known and tried, so much the better. If buying through an advertisement, endeavour to get an unbiased opinion on the working qualities of your prospective purchase before parting with your money, and insist on a trial.

As a beginning, I would suggest including in your purchases a good brood bitch or two. You will then be able later on to breed puppies to augment your pack, and make good your losses, and you may even turn a little money on the sale of surplus stock.

That you are likely to meet with some disappointments in your breeding ventures goes without saying. In that, as in other things, one cannot hope for invariable success, but by considering nothing but really good working stock in the first place you are much less apt to have failures than by buying casually any smart-looking pup that comes along.

Always be on the lookout to purchase anything really good that you may see working with a scratch crowd, and do not set too much value on looks. Handsome is as handsome does in the field, but only *breed* from pure-bred dogs of known ancestry. Mongrels are useless for breeding, though they may themselves be good workers.

Of course, dogs in a Terrier pack need not necessarily be all of the same breed, and indeed the three and a half couple with which the writer enjoyed the best of his sport were a motley crowd, and included three Fox-terriers, a Fox-Irish cross, an Irish " blue Terrier," and a nondescript, the whole topped up with an Irish Water Spaniel. The " blue Terrier " was a small, long-haired, dark, grizzle-and-tan creature, something like an overgrown Yorkshire, and I imagine resembled in nothing the big dogs that are known as Blue Terriers in Ireland to-day. It need hardly be said that a well-matched team of Sealyhams or Fox-terriers will look much smarter than this crowd, and incidentally will confer an air of respectability on their owner, which is an asset in itself. The scratch pack is just mentioned as showing what can be done even with the most slender means.

To revert to the working qualities of Terriers, a good nose has been mentioned as a necessary qualification. For stoat and other hunting, etc., the reason is obvious, but for a badger dog a good nose is also essential. A good dog should be able to decide at once whether an earth is occupied or not ; a quick run through should

BLACK-AND-TAN TERRIER, FROM PICTURE BY SARTORIUS.

settle the matter beyond all doubt. Nothing is more trying than to have a dog go to ground and spend half-an-hour or more poking about in an earth and then come out —" nothing doing ! "

After nose come pluck and endurance, particularly with dogs used for underground work. A dog must not only go into a badger sett, find and bring his badger to bay, but he must stick to him, giving him no rest, it may be for hours on end.

With an indifferent dog it often happens after you have been digging for half an hour or so the dog comes back with the result that the badger, or fox, as the case may be, loses no time in shifting his quarters to some other part of the earth, and all your labour has been in vain ; the whole business must be commenced anew. Needless to say, this sort of thing not only entails great loss of time, but is very discouraging to the men digging.

No hard-and-fast rule can be laid down as to the best size for working Terriers, but other things being equal I should say that the smaller the better. A dog of fifteen or even twelve pounds weight can do all that a big dog can do, and he can move about underground much more easily. Moreover, he is handier to transport, takes up less kennel room, and eats less food, all small matters, no doubt, but worth considering.

FOX AND BADGER DIGGING.

TRAINING AND ENTERING TERRIERS TO FOX AND BADGER.

Opinions differ very considerably as to the age at which a dog should be entered to work underground. Some would have us start a puppy's education at nine months, while others hold that a year and a half is not too old. For myself, I would never put a dog to dangerous game under a year, at any rate. A puppy of nine months old will not put up any sort of a fight with a badger, and if once badly mauled may be cured of badger hunting for good and all.

Puppies of eight months or over, however, may with advantage be taken out to watch the older dogs working, and if opportunity offers, to indulge in worrying a cub, or a dead fox or badger. In this way they become familiar with the business of hunting, and are not scared to death with unaccustomed sights and sounds when their turn for work does arrive later on.

When taking any young dog out for the first time you should handle him very quietly. Do not shove him into a hole to an accompaniment of yells and horn-blowings, for nothing is more calculated to scare him out of his wits. Rather, lead him quietly up to the mouth of the hole where the work is proceeding, and let him listen to the barking of the old dog or dogs inside.

At first he will probably be perfectly indifferent to the whole business, but after a time or two his interest will be aroused, and you may expect to see him venture his nose a foot or two inside. You should still make no effort to press him ; remember it is the unseen and unknown danger that is always terrifying, and your pup will do much better if allowed to investigate matters cautiously in his own way.

· The next day you take him out he will probably go in further, perhaps right up to where the other dogs are working, but will soon come out again to see where you

OLD FOILER.

TROILUS.

SHARPER.

THREE GENERATIONS.

are. When you have got to this point it is only a matter
of time. If the youngster is going to be any good he
will soon be taking his place with his elders, and if he is
not get rid of him, for he will prove but a hindrance to
sport.

THE BADGER.

This interesting beast, though living underground like
the fox, resembles him in no other particular. Slower,
heavier, and less cunning, his habits and ways of life
differ entirely from those of his red neighbour. He is
almost, if not quite, harmless to farmers and game
preservers, and may live long in one place without
anyone being aware of his existence. He certainly does
dig out a nest of young rabbits now and then, and some
of his detractors have even accused him of favouring an
egg diet, but I think we may return a verdict of " not
proven " on that count. His dietary normally consists
of roots, beetles, grubs, and such humble fare ; he is also
a great destroyer of wasps' nests, which he digs up for the
sake of the larvæ, of which he is extremely fond, and for
this service alone he is deserving of our gratitude.

The badger is entirely nocturnal in its habits, and
is very seldom met with abroad in the day time, and for
this reason there are many country people who have
never seen one. Very occasionally a badger may be
found " lying rough "—i.e., curled up in some hedge-
bottom or the dry corner of an orchard, but I am inclined
to think that this is due to his having been scared away
from his earth by some passing dog or person, or by
the placing of a trap near the entrance thereof. Badgers
are amongst the most wary and suspicious of living
creatures, and the smallest thing will suffice to keep
them away from an earth, or, once in it, prevent them
from coming out again.

The badger is believed to live for from twelve to
fifteen years. The sow is in season in the month of
October or November, but the time she carries her young
is still a matter of doubt, and probably varies very

greatly. There have been several well-authenticated cases of badgers in captivity giving birth to young twelve or fifteen months after capture, with no possibility of their having been mated during the interval. The usual number of cubs in a litter is three or four.

Cases of albinism in badgers, though rare, are by no means unknown. Personally, I have come across but two white badgers in a long period of years.

The badger is a desperate fighter, and a much more redoubtable adversary than his neighbour the fox, as nearly every hunter knows to his cost. Many, alas, are the losses of brave and hardy Terriers as the result of encounters with this terrible antagonist.

As with a fox, the case or difficulty of taking a badger depends on the nature of the earth, but in every case there is plenty of hard work to be done' for both dogs and men.

THE FOX.

In England, where foxes are strictly preserved for Foxhounds, the Terrier owner will rarely have to do with the red robber, unless indeed he constitutes himself runner to some pack of hounds, in which case his services may be requisitioned fairly frequently. In the Highlands of Scotland, however, and in many parts of Ireland, where no pack of Foxhounds exists, Reynard may be taken by any and every means. Thief and poacher, plunderer of poultry yards, and destroyer of game, who kills for the pleasure of killing, he is given no quarter, and to slay him is regarded as doing a service to the community.

The dietary of the fox is very varied, and includes, besides game and poultry (and in the mountainous districts new-born lambs), such tit-bits as rats, moles, and squirrels, numbers of which he will stow away in his larder, particularly at the time when his vixen is nursing her cubs. The fox is supposed to live about twelve or fourteen years.

THE LEWES BADGER-DIGGING PARTY.

MR. JEFF SALES, MR. H. NASH, AND MR. H.
POOLE WITH THEIR "BAG."

The vixen comes in season about the New Year, and carries her young nine weeks, the usual number at a birth being four to six, though larger litters occur sometimes.

The young fox-cubs are fed by their mother up to the age of six months or so, after which they commence to hunt for themselves.

The digging out of a fox in small low-country earths is generally a pretty simple matter, but in mountainous districts, where the great rocky fastnesses have been held by fox and badger for centuries, the affair is not nearly so simple. A dog may get up to his fox almost immediately, but cannot keep him in one place, the first sound of digging overhead serving to send Master Reynard scuttling to some other part of his castle, and it may require three or four good dogs to corner a fox in a place of this kind.

The fox, contrary to general belief, is a very courageous animal, and defends himself with much fury when attacked, often inflicting very severe wounds on his adversaries. The bite of a fox, moreover, is very poisonous, and no time should be lost in washing and treating wounds of this nature.

THE EARTH.

While foxes and badgers both have their homes below ground they differ in this much—that whereas a fox will frequently change his abode a badger, if undisturbed, never does. Indeed, it is probable that some of the larger earths in various parts of the country have been continuously inhabited for centuries.

It is not always apparent at first sight whether an earth is the home of fox or badger. If the footprints are visible in the soft earth or mud, there is no room for further doubt on the matter ; the marks of the two animals are entirely different, and once seen cannot be confounded. The fox's footprint resembles that of a small dog, and has but four toes, while in the case of the badger the marks made by the long claws appear quite detached from the ball of the foot, and there are five toes. Other sure signs of badger are the little pits which he digs in the vicinity of his earth, in which to deposit his excrement, and which in the summer season frequently attract many bluebottles.

Amongst other evidences of the existence of badgers may be mentioned the large mound of soil accumulated at the mouth of the earth, and the smooth well-marked path by which he invariably enters and leaves. The entrance to a badger sett may be in an open field or in a hillside, in full view of the surrounding country, whilst a fox much prefers his front door to be hidden in the undergrowth. It is not very uncommon to find a fox and a badger occupying the same earth, and the two have been frequently taken at the same dig. Some badger setts of great antiquity form veritable catacombs under the face of the hill. The entrances to these places are as a rule numerous, wide, and deep, evidence of generations of skilful and tireless effort on the part of the occupants. To handle a badger in such a fortress is always a difficult, and often an impossible, undertaking.

The interior arrangement of a badger earth is as interesting as variable, but all appear to be constructed on the same general principle of a large central chamber, from which run several galleries, and out of which also runs a narrow twisting passage, sometimes up, sometimes down, terminating in a room large enough to accommodate two, three, or more badgers. This is the castle keep, so to speak, and is the last refuge of the garrison, and where the final melee generally takes place. Of course, in the century-old strongholds before mentioned, there will be many chambers and many galleries all communicating with one another, and at varying depths.

In conclusion, it may be said that one never knows how much work is ahead when one commences digging. You may come up to your dog and badger within a couple or three feet of the surface, or they may be eight or ten feet down.

REDTOP, FOX-TERRIER.

BADGER DIGGING.

PERSONNEL AND EQUIPMENT.

Three things are above all necessary to success in badger digging—good dogs, good diggers, and a good ear. Add to these a good slice of patience and a capacity for suffering disappointment without becoming unduly discouraged, and you have it all.

I have already remarked on the importance of having hard, well-entered dogs. With dogs that come out of the earth every half-hour, you may as well go home, for you will never handle a badger in a week, except by demolishing the whole earth, in which case that locality is lost to you for sport in the future. No fox or badger will go there again for many a long day, if ever.

Next to good dogs come good diggers. Lazy, idle fellows, or bad workmen who don't know their business, spoil many a promising hunt.

Except in very large, difficult places, where it may be necessary to sink two, or even three, trenches, or where the work is so extensive as to require relays of diggers, two or three good men will do all you want. But they must be keen, and have a real taste for the work.

The late war afforded excellent practice in trench digging to some of us, and many old soldiers are first-rate hands with the pick and shovel ; they are generally good sportsmen, too.

The idle loafer picked up outside the village pub is, as a rule, useless, and spends most of his time mopping his brow and trying to get a pull at the beer-jar ; and, talking of beer, it is well to make a hard-and-fast rule that refreshment is only for those who earn it, and not for spectators.

With some Terrier clubs it is the custom to take round a " cap " after the dig, to pay the diggers and meet other casual expenses. One should have an understanding with the diggers that they are to be paid so much per day (or half a day, as the case may be), with a bonus for every full-grown beast taken, or else to divide the cap money, less a percentage. Personally, I much prefer the former plan, but much depends on the class of men with whom you have to deal.

Finally, a good ear is important, that you may readily ascertain the exact spot below which the dog and badger are situated, and so commence your digging operations in the right place. Nothing is more discouraging to men than to find, after half-an-hour's work on a hot day, that their labour has been in vain, and a fresh start has to be made somewhere else,

EQUIPMENT.

With regard to the question of equipment generally, this should be kept as simple as possible ; a multitude of fancy tools and appliances is very inconvenient to transport, and generally unnecessary.

A couple of spades, a pick or two with adze-shaped heads (such as are known as " twobills " or " diggers " in some parts of the country), a crowbar, a shovel, a chopper or hatchet for cutting roots, and a badger tongs are the essentials. There are also one or two little special tools known as spuds and scrapers, which are useful in small places. A stout canvas sack, ventilated with brass eyelet holes, and having a draw string and strap and buckle at the neck, is also required to put your quarry in when captured.

THE DIG.

Being now fully equipped with the necessary dogs and tools, and attended by a couple of good spade men, we may take the field. The first thing to do, having acquired information as to the position of the earths you mean to work, is to make a thorough inspection of the ground, ascertain what openings there are, and whether they have been recently used, and by what animals. The earth will commonly be situated on the side of a hill, with entrances above and below, and some men hold

WIRE-HAIRED FOX-TERRIERS MOLE HUNTING.

At length the Mole begins to move the
surface soil, and the dogs back and get
ready to spring and kill.

that the dog should always be put in at the lower hole, while others favour that on the higher ground. There is really nothing whatever in it ; it is purely a matter of chance. Just loose your best and most reliable dog and leave matters to him, and he will soon decide for himself which passage will lead him most quickly to his foe. If the earth is unoccupied a good dog will lose no time in letting you see that such is the case, for he will leave the earth altogether and go hunting for a better place

If, on the other hand, your dog goes to ground and remains there, listen attentively at the mouth of the hole for the first sounds of combat, and then cheer your dog on with all the power of your lungs. After a few minutes you may expect a period of silence, and then the fight will commence anew in some other part of the earth. If the place is a big one you may now slip another dog to assist, but not if there is a likelihood of the dogs fighting each other. A dog and bitch are best suited for this job, as there is then no danger of a row. After two or three sparring matches and running fights things will probably settle down below, and then, with your ear to the ground or against a crowbar driven in, you must endeavour to arrive at the spot immediately above the fight, and commence digging.

As has been indicated in a previous chapter, it is not always easy to know at first sight what animal you have got to deal with in an earth, whether fox or badger ; the external evidences are not invariably unmistakable, but when you know your dogs their manner of working will generally not leave you long in doubt.

Having engaged in two or three lively duels with the dogs in different chambers and passages, the badger as a rule sets up pretty quickly, and the continuous baying of the Terriers in one place leaves little doubt as to where digging operations must begin. With a fox the procedure will be much the same where the earth is small, but in a big working, where he has lots of room, things are somewhat different. After the first sounds of warfare, which will only last a few minutes, there will be a rush and a scuffle, and then silence. After a while out will come your dog in great excitement, nose down, convinced that his adversary has given him the slip and gone away, but almost immediately back he will go, and after a few more minutes' exploring you will hear him find his fox afresh and recommence the fight. You now start digging, but at the first few strokes of the pick off goes Reynard again, and it may be an hour, with two or three dogs after him, before he is finally cornered.

Another useful test in cases of uncertainty is the examination of the dog's claws as soon as he shows up ; there will often be found the hairs of the hunted animal sticking to them. Fox fur particularly clings tenaciously to a dog's feet, and the odour of fox is also sometimes quite noticeable about his mouth.

When baying a badger most dogs give tongue more continuously than when dealing with a fox. With the latter animal their inclination seems to be to close with their adversary and to bring matters to a head as soon as possible. One can still hear the fight going on, of course, but not a succession of barks—rather a muffled sound of fierce and bloody combat, and no sparring.

In hunting a fox underground care must be taken to stop all holes but one, and have that well watched, otherwise he will surely bolt when you least expect it ; but with a badger these precautions are usually omitted, for a badger seldom bolts, but fights it out to the bitter end, or if he does mean to take to the country he usually does so as soon as the dog is put in and before digging operations are started.

At a recent meet of the Bideford Badger Club a badger was twice bolted from two different earths without a spade being put to the ground, and gave an excellent run of an hour or so, with all the Terriers and the whole field after him, before he was finally lost.

Before commencing digging it is most important to form an opinion as to the direction of the line of the passage or gallery in which your dog is, so that you may sink your trench at right angles to it. You will thus make sure of cutting the gallery somewhere, otherwise

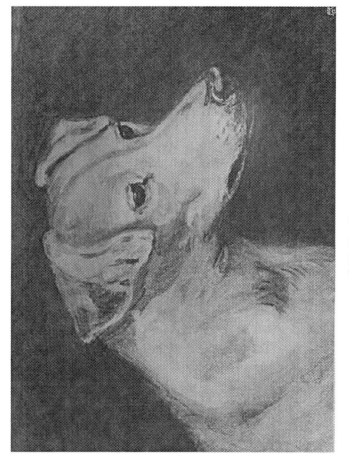

ROY, FOX-TERRIER.

you may be excavating in a direction parallel to it, and put in a lot of useless work before you find your mistake.

Always insist on your men cutting a good wide trench while they are about it, and see that they maintain the width as they go down ; there is nothing more annoying than to see men poking about in the bottom of a narrow trench, with no room to use their tools. It is in these little details that the keen and experienced digger evidences his value ; he knows his job and understands what you are trying to do, while the casual labourer is just working for his pay, and is more or less in the dark as to what is really required of him.

As the work goes on, and you are getting nearer the scene of combat, caution your men to go carefully with their picks, lest they suddenly come upon the dogs and injure them.

The din of battle becomes louder and clearer every minute, and then perhaps there will be a horrid noise of a dog in agony, and one of your gallant little warriors will appear at the mouth of the hole badly torn and mauled. He should be immediately taken up, put on a lead, and his wounds washed and dressed, while another dog is despatched to take his place at the front.

The diggers will now be working fast and furious and louder and clearer sounds the baying of the dogs. Presently a stroke of the spade lays bare the passage where the fight is in progress, and if you are lucky you may be close enough to handle your beast without more ado. If, however, dogs and badger are still out of reach, stop any other holes leading into the trench, open up the gallery till you can get your tongs to bear, and drag the badger out, dogs and all. See that your sack is held ready, and after the dogs have been taken up, pop him in. A sacked badger should not be left on the ground, or he will tear his way out of the bag. The bag should rather be suspended to the branch of a tree if it has to be left for any time.

If dogs and badger are, say, ten or twelve feet from the trench, when you reach the gallery, it is best to get the dogs out if possible. Clear everybody away from the trench, and enjoin silence. Then commence digging right over the place where the badger is. Having no dog to contend with, and hearing the digging going on above him, the badger will generally bolt into the trench himself, where he must be seized before he has time to get back. Sometimes you may lose your badger at the last moment, so to speak, through his digging his way through into some neighbouring gallery, and making his escape.

Badgers are also very prone, if they get a chance, to earth themselves in—that is, they throw up a solid wall of earth behind them, and between themselves and the dog, blinding the latter, and completely blocking the passage, and then adding to the thickness of this as they go along. Hard-bitten, experienced dogs seldom allow time for this operation on the part of Master Brock, but with young dogs, or those not so hard, this trick sometimes succeeds, and delays matters considerably, as even a good dog going down after may have considerable difficulty in fresh finding his badger through a three-foot wall of earth.

Sometimes badgers are already earthed in when one arrives at the scene of operations (probably having been scared by some dog or person just before), and then it takes a good dog to get on terms with them. Occasionally a badger will dig himself out of the earth altogether and take to the country, but this happens but rarely.

Always be careful to fill in your trenches, and make good any damage before leaving the earth. Foxes and badgers will not resort to a place that has been left in ruins ; and remember that it is only by courtesy of the owner or occupier of land that one hunts at all, so that anything that is likely to cause them loss or annoyance must be avoided.

BADGER HUNTING AT NIGHT.

This is a branch of the sport which is very little practised, and for good reason, for it entails being abroad at most unconscionable hours of the night, and stumbling and falling about in the dark, to say nothing of frightening cattle and sheep, etc.

Indeed, unless there are badgers close to where you live or are staying with your dogs, the game is hardly worth the candle.

The procedure, which is simple, is as follows :—

On a fine night, with a good moon, a careful and, if possible, experienced watcher secretes himself just before dark in some place where he can obtain a clear view of the earth and down wind of it. He must be very patient, for he may have a long and dreary vigil, and he must never for one instant take his eyes off the mouth of the hole. If he does, that will be just the time that Master Brock chooses to slip out unobserved.

Badgers are extraordinarily cautious and suspicious creatures, and never leave their earth without waiting for some considerable time at the entrance, listening and sniffing the wind to detect the presence of an enemy. The snapping of a twig or the rustle of a leaf at this time is sufficient to put them down for the rest of the evening. Even after coming out, they will often remain playing about outside for some considerable time before they set forth on their nightly prowl, and will be ready to pop back again at the first sight or sound of danger.

If, and when, the observer sees the badgers emerge from their dwelling, and disappear into the woods, he gives them twenty minutes' law so that they may get well away, and then fastens a sack or large purse net in the mouth of the hole, pegging it lightly down, and fastens the draw string to a stump or tree. Having done this he stops any holes, which are not bagged, with strong faggots previously prepared, and signals the huntsman by whistle or flashlight that all is ready.

The Master then unkennels his dogs, and draws round in a wide circle until he hits the trail of the badgers. As soon as the dogs settle on the line and commence to give tongue, the badgers realise that all is not well and make for home at their best pace, the hunt stumbling along behind as best they can.

If Brock is being pressed pretty closely, he will generally dash straight into the sack on arrival at the earth, but if he has time to investigate, he may scent danger, and give it the go by. For this reason it is well for the watcher to remain on guard, and when he sees the badger approaching the earth he should show himself and yell. This will generally have the effect of hastening matters, and leave Master Brock no time for thought. As soon as the badger is bagged, the watcher runs in and makes all secure, the hunt comes up, and all is over but the final whoo-hoop !

One can, of course, dispense with the services of a watcher, if need be, but in that case one must not bag the earth or commence to draw before eleven o'clock or midnight, and even then you cannot be sure that your badger has gone away, and may spend half the night hunting for nothing.

No earth stopping must be done at any of the entrances to the sett before the badger comes out. All preparations, moreover, should be made the previous day, and no one should be allowed near the earth on the day of the hunt, for if he hears people moving about over his head Brocky will remain at home, and so may you for all the sport you will get.

OTTER HUNTING.

Of all the varieties of Terrier sport I know of, this is at once the most enjoyable and the most disappointing. It is not often that one is successful, but when one is there is no sport like it.

Otter hunting with Terriers must, of course, only be practised in countries where there are no Otterhounds. and where the otter is considered as vermin, to be

Miss GUEST'S RANÊE, Wire-Haired Terrier.

exterminated by trap and gun or any other means. Waters hunted by regular packs of hounds, or which are within the borders of their countries, should never be touched.

In England practically the whole country is divided up amongst the various otter packs, so that the huntable streams are closed to Terrier men ; but in many parts of Ireland and Scotland there are no Otterhounds, and *lutra vulgaris* is classed as an outlaw, and may be hunted and killed by anyone and anyhow.

Of the otter and his nature little need be said save that he is far more abundant than most country people know or are willing to believe. I have frequently killed otters in districts where the oldest inhabitants have assured me that they had never heard of the existence of such an animal.

Indeed, one can safely say that there be few rivers and streams in these islands that are not occasionally visited by one or more of them, but owing to their entirely nocturnal habits they are rarely seen by ordinary folk.

Otters are great travellers, and will cover many miles of country, moving from one water to another, particularly during the breeding season or when they have been disturbed by hounds.

An otter that has been hunted and made good his escape will not as a rule return to those waters for two or three weeks or more.

The home or hiding-place of an otter is termed his " holt," or in Ireland more commonly called his " den." It is usually a hole or burrow under the bank, or under the roots of an old tree, with the entrance under water. Sometimes there is also an above-water entrance hidden in the undergrowth, and very often there are vent holes, which are of great assistance to questing Terriers in discovering Master Otter's whereabouts.

Otters are constantly changing their abode, the plentitude or scarcity of food deciding their place of residence for the time being. They are also very variable in their choice of a dwelling, and on occasion will make use of any hole, natural or artificial, which appears to afford safe hiding and dry lying, for, in spite of their aquatic habits, otters like to sleep dry and warm during the day. I have found otters lying up in old walls, in the stonework of bridges, in the basement of a disused house, in rabbit burrows, and very frequently in drains. Otters will also lie out in reed beds, rough grass, and hedges, in fine weather.

Of the breeding habits of the otter very little appears to be known. Bitches with young have been met with all through the spring and summer months, and the period during which they carry their young seems likewise to vary considerably, though about six weeks would appear to be the average.

The food of the otter is principally fish, of which he takes heavy toll, and wastes much more than he eats ; but a great many other articles of diet figure on his menu, too. Frogs, voles, young waterhens, and ducklings may all be partaken of.

The first otter I ever hunted and killed made his presence known by decimating a neighbouring farmer's flock of ducks.

Otters frequent the smallest as well as the largest ponds and watercourses, and it is in the former that the hunter stands the best chance of success. On wide, deep rivers and in lakes of any size hunting is impracticable even with full-sized hounds.

OTTER DOGS AND THEIR TRAINING.

Before we go any further it may be said right away that in hunting with a small pack of Terriers it will be idle to expect them to swim and kill their otter unaided. The spear must be used, and freely, if results are to be looked for. I know that there is strong prejudice in England against the use of the spear on humanitarian grounds, but it is merely prejudice. The spear is surer and not more cruel than the gun, and much less so than the odious trap, wherein the wretched animal lingers in agony till found by his captor and beaten to death with a stick. Moreover, the spear has been used in comparatively recent years by some of our best sportsmen, and I have it on the authority of men who hunted with him that the late " Otter " Davies (than whom no better sportsman and gentleman ever carried a horn), used his spear frequently to save hounds in heavy water, or whenever the circumstances of the chase demanded.

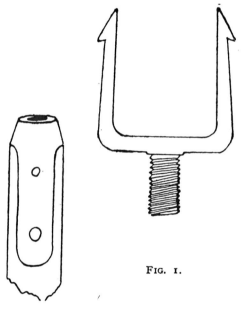

FIG. 1.

Of otter spears, or otter "grains" as they are called, there are several patterns, but we need only deal with two—viz., the two-pronged barbed spear, Fig. 1, and the pitchfork pattern, Fig. 2. The latter, which has long, straight, and barbless points, is the easier and cheaper to make, and is quite efficient, though possibly not so sure of its hold as the barbed spear. Either may be made with a detachable head to screw into a socket in the pole if desired.

The pole or shaft should be of well-seasoned wood— ash is best—eight to ten feet long, and perfectly straight, with a slight taper at each end. It must also be of

sufficient strength and thickness to allow of it being
used as a jumping pole for crossing unwadeable dykes
and drains.

Spear heads can be turned out
by any blacksmith, and are best
made of soft steel as less likely to
break, and when they become
blunted by contact with rocks are
easily sharpened up again by means
of a file.

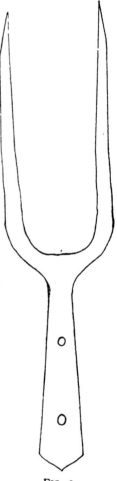

Good spear shafts are sometimes difficult to obtain. The otter
poles sold by sports firms are too
short, and useless for our purpose,
but long boat-hook staves, procur-
able from boat builders and ship-
yards, can often be made to serve,
as also can old Navy boarding
pikes.

The first step towards successful
otter hunting is the training and
entering of your dogs. Few
Terriers have a natural and in-
stinctive love for water, and a
great many appear to be born with
a great aversion to it. All, however, can be brought with a little
patience to take to the chilly
element readily enough when in
search of prey. Never on any
account throw a young dog into
the water. Let him get over his
fears and dislikes quietly and in
his own way. Encourage him to

FIG. 2.

hunt and to scratch at the rat-holes in the bank,
getting down into the water yourself at the shallow
places to search underneath. Also cross the stream
from time to time, either by wading or jumping with a
pole, and encourage him to follow you. If there are
old dogs in the party, they will, of course, swim

Miss GUEST'S PACK OF SPORTING TERRIERS.

backwards and forwards readily, and seeing them will soon give the youngsters confidence. It rarely takes more than a day or two to get over this preliminary school‐ing, after that the youngster will at least follow his seniors anywhere.

The next move, and by no means so simple, is enter‐ing to otter. The best and most successful method, if you can manage it, is to acquire the services of an old Otterhound or Foxhound who has been used for otter, and let him act as guide and tutor to your pack. It is seldom, however, that one can come by such a treasure. Masters of Otterhounds do not sell their good hounds, and only part with their worst in consideration of many shekels of silver. The poor man must therefore forego this luxury, and see what he can do for himself, making eyes and intelligence take the place of nose.

The first thing, then, is to find out by persistent inquiries from farmers, millers, gamekeepers, river poachers, and anyone else who is likely to know whether an otter has been recently seen or heard of in the neigh‐bourhood, and where. Proceed to the location with your pack, the earlier the better, and with your com‐panions search carefully every yard of the river bank or sandy spots where the " seal " or foot-mark of the otter might lie. Also keep your eye lifting for his " spraints " or dung on the stones in mid-stream, and if you find either of these traces you will at least know that there is an otter somewhere about, and can proceed with more confidence.

Now work on in the direction the otter was travelling, leaving no hole or root unsearched, and cheer and encourage your dogs to hunt all the time, and have your spears in constant readiness for use. If you are lucky you may eventually arrive at the otter's " holt " and eject him with the aid of a Terrier. If that otter is speared and killed while the dogs are hunting him, half your troubles are over. Your dogs now know (1) what an otter smells like, and (2) that there is good sport to be found in hunting him. The rest is just work and experience.

OTTER HUNTING.—The Hunt.

For otter hunting one needs at least five spearmen, and not less than three couples of dogs, the more the better so long as they will hunt and swim.

The early morning is undoubtedly the best time for this sport ; in fact, the earlier the better. " On the water by daybreak " is a good rule, always supposing that you can find companions ardent and keen enough to take the field with you at that hour. The object of being abroad so early is to pick up the drag or trail of the animal as he returns home from his night's fishing, and, by being close behind him, have a fresh scent to follow. If you wait till the sun is up and the dew is off the grass, the line will be stale, or lost altogether, and then it becomes a matter of " ratting " from one known " holt " to the next in the hope of finding an otter at home.

When drawing for an otter, dogs and field should be divided, half taking one bank and half the other. Then slowly draw up stream, every likely looking spot both on and under the bank should be well rummaged out with the pole.

If the dogs hit the drag of an otter care must at once be taken to ascertain in which direction he is moving, which will be indicated by his seal where he has passed over any soft earth or mud, and also by his spraints, noting whether they be on the up-stream or down-stream side of the rocks. One may have a long way to go from where one first strikes the trail of an otter to the place where he lies, as these creatures travel many miles in a night in search of food ; but, on the other hand, your quarry may be close under your feet, and no pains must be spared to see that you do not pass over him.

If, and when, the dogs find the otter's holt, a Terrier is put in, and if necessary digging is resorted to till such time as the otter is persuaded to bolt, or is " put down," as the term goes.

REDTOP. ROSA. REDSTART. AMORA. ARDENT. ROY. RACER. ATTICA. . DINAH.

ROSTER. RADIX.

A SPORTING XI.

Immediately an otter is " put down " or " marked in," the hunters (who should have been instructed in their duties beforehand) must divide themselves Two run as fast as their legs will carry them up stream to the nearest shallows, where they can be sure of viewing the quarry should he pass that way, while two more run down stream and take up a similar position below. The fifth man—where there are five—will be the huntsman, and remain with the dogs, and to him, as a rule, is most of the work and most of the fun. An otter once headed will generally endeavour to hide under the bank, with just his nose showing above water, and one may sometimes see and spear him so, but more often there will be a good many dashes up and down the pool, with long disappearances under water, before one gets on terms with him.

Any casual followers should be told off, some to the upper stickle, some to the lower, and the remainder surround the pool where the otter is, and look for him " venting " or getting out on to the bank.

Whenever the otter vents—that is, comes to the surface—the person seeing him holloas " Tally Ho ! " or " Heu Gaze ! " The huntsman cheers his dogs to the spot, and endeavours to impale the otter on his spear, while the dogs strive to seize him. When tackled by a dog in the water an otter usually dives, otter and dog going down together locked fast in each other's grip. Sometimes in strong waters the dog never comes up again alive, so it behoves a Terrier huntsman to be quick and handy with the grains and save his dogs.

Should the otter, as often happens, be already dashing up stream full speed, the foremost hunters must get ahead of him at all costs before making their stickle, the remainder of the hunt following on, and seeking to confine the otter in the smallest huntable space of water.

Should the otter dash down stream and succeed in forcing the lower " stickle," the hunters whom he has passed must notify the others by a loud " Gone away, tally ! " and go full speed down stream to cut him off at the next shallows, the huntsman following with his dogs, while the men at the upper stickle move down to the place vacated by the two first, and so on till you get your otter again encompassed in a small stretch of water.

Of course, each hunter tries to use his spear when opportunity offers, but on no account must those stationed at a stickle leave their places or relax their vigilance for one moment. They must keep their eyes on the water just in front of them, and their spears in the water.

When an otter is speared do not attempt any stunts, such as hoisting him out of the water, etc. Hold him down and drown him. Good dogs are scarce, and otters can inflict terrible punishment.

Otters defend themselves with great courage and much ferocity when attacked by Terriers in an earth or drain, and no animal of its size is capable of giving a more deadly bite. For this reason it is inadvisable to put young and untried dogs up to an otter till they have been previously entered to fox or badger.

The scent of the otter is very strong, surpassing in strength even that of the fox. Yet Terriers seem to take less kindly to it than that of any animal which one hunts, and it is for this reason that the trailing and finding an otter may well prove a hopeless task without the assistance of a well-entered dog or two.

I believe in doing everything possible to interest waterside dwellers in one's sport, and getting them to supply one with information as to the movements and resorts of otters. Pay as generously as you can for information which leads to a find, but on no account give anything for that which proves sterile.

In dealing with country people generally it is well to choose your company with some tact and discretion. Too close an acquaintance with the local poachers, for instance, may get you " in bad " with gamekeepers and land-owners.

In Ireland, information is always forthcoming, and wonderful accounts will reach you of the size, ferocity, and depredations of the "water dog," but most of them must be taken *cum grano salis*, and it takes no little experience to enable one to sift the wheat from the chaff.

I have found it a useful practice when hunting to take an opportunity of explaining to casual followers, boys and others, the principles and objects of the chase, and to instruct them a little in the habits of the quarry. Thus, when I come upon the well-marked seal of an otter, I call the boys round and show it to them, so they may know what it looks like, and see in what it differs from the footmark of a dog, etc. By this means you interest the youngsters and make them observant and keen.

Unquestionably the best season for otter-hunting with Terriers is in the winter, when there is snow on the ground, as they may then be traced very easily to their den. One must, however, be prepared to withstand a good deal of cold and hardship if one takes the field at this time of the year, and consider the possibility of colds and rheumatics to follow.

On some small streams, of course, long rubber boots reaching to the thigh may be worn, but as often as not one gets " over the top " even in these.

In some places where the coast is wild and unfrequented otters often resort to the caves and rocks by the seashore, and food being plentiful and easily caught, they often attain to a great size.

Shore otters live either in some cave with a dry hole or ledge at the far end, or in a heap of rocks. From such places it is often very hard to eject them, and they cannot be hunted in the usual way.

The best method of dealing with them is having put in one or two Terriers, keep the remainder of the pack a few yards away, and between the otter's hole and the sea. If and when he bolts, loose the whole pack, and get in with your spear and finish him before he can do any damage if you can.

Shore hunting should only be undertaken at low tide. At high water the bolt hole will be most likely submerged, and, moreover, you will not be able to get about over the rocks and round the cliffs.

Another method of taking otters where the water is deep, and there are no shallows where one can form a stickle, is with the aid of nets. Having marked your otter to ground, or having otherwise reason to believe that an otter is in a certain spot, a net weighted with lead along one side, and attended by a man at each end, is spread a short distance up stream, and right across from bank to bank, while a similar net occupies a position below. Then the otter being put down can be hunted in the space between the two nets till speared or killed by the dogs. He will only try to drive through the nets as a last resource.

It is most essential that the nets should completely block the whole passage, as an otter will take advantage of the smallest gap.

Nets should be of strong twine, and about 2-in. mesh.

Old fishing-nets, which can be bought cheaply, do well enough for this purpose.

In conclusion, I may say that one never knows until one has tried what dogs may prove useful for otter-hunting. I have known common Sheepdogs take to the business as to the manner born, and the best dog I ever owned for this work was an Irish Water Spaniel Indeed, except for the fact that he ran mute, he was as good as any Otterhound I ever knew, and would swim all day long, searching every hole under the bank, and frequently diving under water.

Of course, small dogs like Working Terriers are at a great disadvantage as compared with long-legged hounds, and if one were making a speciality of this form of sport, the larger dogs one could get the better, but it has been assumed that the Terrier man's little pack will be kept for all round work, and otter-hunting will only be taken as a side line.

THE FOX-TERRIER RACER.

of Bickford's fuse in one's pocket. One of these lit and shoved into the hole will generally shift him. The dogs must be kept away from the bury while this is going on, not alone to give the stoat a chance to bolt, but so that they shall not get powder smoke in their noses.

When " hounds " check or run out of scent the hunts-man must come to their assistance, and endeavour to get a view of the hunted animal, searching carefully along the top of the hedge, or the lower branches of an overhanging tree, in the ivy of a wall, or anywhere else that may furnish a hiding place, for our little friend is an active climber, and will take refuge in the most unexpected places.

If you catch sight of the stoat up a tree, and the branches are fairly bare, a shout will generally bring him down ; but if he has any cover to hide him, you may have quite a job to dislodge the little beast, though he will generally respond to pelting with clods of earth, etc., in time.

It is marvellous how a stoat will get away from dogs. I have seen one more than once fall off a roof or branch of a tree right into the jaws of the waiting pack, and then go clear away. Once caught, however, a stoat, unlike a rat, never seems to inflict any punishment on the dog, but is killed instantly.

If you are hunting a stoat and lose him it will be useless to look for him again next day, for he will have gone clear out of the country. They are great travellers, and never fail to go while the going is good.

RATS AND RATTING.

There are two species of rats found in these islands, the black and the brown (or grey). The former, known as the old English black rat, is now scarce, and localised in its distribution. A few colonies still remain on the East Coast of England, and in some of the dock-yards, but elsewhere the larger and fiercer brown rat has driven him out. Black rats are still common on board ship.

The black rat is a smaller, prettier, and cleaner creature than the brown, but is almost, if not quite, as destructive, and in addition has the unenviable reputation of being the disseminator of the deadly bubonic and pleuro-pneumonic plagues.

The brown, or as he is sometimes called, the Hanoverian rat, is well known and cordially detested everywhere. A filthy and repulsive brute, he is far and away the worst animal plague that we have, not alone in numbers, which are said to exceed one hundred millions in Great Britain alone, but also by reason of the damage which he does and the quantity of foodstuffs which he consumes or destroys.

It has been estimated that the value of this latter amounts to forty million (£40,000,000) pounds sterling per annum.

The only good points about rats which I have ever discovered is the pleasure which the killing of them affords to dogs and men. Let us make the most of it.

Of ratting with Terriers we can say that there are two principal methods—(1) with ferrets, and (2) without.

The former is undoubtedly the more prolific of results, but involves the keeping and looking after ferrets, and the sometimes objectionable necessity of breaking your dogs to them. Dogs that have been broken to ferrets will sometimes refuse to hunt stoat and otter, though it is difficult to see what connection there can be between the scent of stoat or ferret and that of otter, the last-named animal having none of the fetid and unpleasant odour of the other two.

Of the keeping and working of ferrets much has been written by abler pens than mine, and there are several excellent handbooks published which deal with the subject exhaustively. I, therefore, do not propose to venture more than a few general remarks which may be of interest to beginners. First of all I would say that though ferrets can be kept anywhere, it always pays in the long run to have a large, roomy, and properly

AMORA, WIRE-HAIRED TERRIER.

STOAT HUNTING.

This little-known and little-practised branch of the phase is, I think, quite the best Terrier hunting to be had in these islands. Indeed, I question whether for real sport and variety of incident it can be beaten by any other foot-hunting whatever.

The stoat—erroneously known as the weasel in Ireland—is one of the commonest of our smaller carnivoræ; it is also unquestionably one of the most destructive, taking heavy toll of game, both fur and feather, and not disdaining an occasional visit to the poultry yard.

Blessed with truly wonderful scenting powers, the stoat follows its prey with an energy and persistence unequalled by any other beast of prey. He will doggedly follow a hare or rabbit, hunting their line like a hound, till the poor beast, worn out by terror and fatigue, lies down and waits its doom, when the cruel little tyrant of the woods seizes it behind the ear, severing the artery, and sucks its life-blood, the victim as a rule making little or no resistance.

The stoat is widely distributed throughout the whole Northern temperate zone, and is common in most European countries. In Northern climates, including Scotland, the colour of the fur, which is a rich brown, changes in winter to white, but in England and Ireland there is little or no change of pelage throughout the year. The costly and much-prized ermine fur is but the stoat in Northern winter dress. The female stoat is in season about the month of December, and the young, four or five in number, are born nine weeks later. Sometimes there are two litters in the year, one in spring and one in autumn.

The stoat is perhaps the boldest animal of its size in the world, and will attack creatures many times larger than itself. They have even been known to attack a man when interfered with. The female also defends her young with the greatest gallantry.

c

Though the stoat is abroad in the country at all times of the year, it is only in the mating season—*i.e.*, the late winter and early spring—that he can be hunted with much chance of success. True, one may find a stoat in the hedgerows at other times of the year, but it is only during the period before-mentioned that he regularly ventures far afield. For the rest of the time he sticks pretty much to woodlands and thick cover.

Stoat hunting where there are many rabbit holes is hopeless, as your quarry is everlastingly going to ground, and affords no more sport that a vulgar rat. On the other hand, if the country is fairly clear of rabbit holes, he often gives a great hunt, and may take you for miles before the dogs finally kill him.

Some dogs, particularly those that have kept broken to ferrets, will not hunt stoat at all, and it is for this reason that I am averse to breaking Working Terriers to ferrets, if it can be avoided. Most Terriers, however, take kindly enough to the sport, and soon become very keen.

The best places to draw for stoat are rough hedge-rows, old walls, gorse, thorny places along the banks of streams and ditches, etc. You will probably account for several rats while seeking the nobler game, and sometimes it is not easy to know whether it is a rat or a stoat that is afoot, but with a little experience the manner of the dogs' working, and the fact that their hackles rise when on a stoat, will soon put you right.

The chase, once fairly started, is most exciting and full of variety, as the little ruffian is as twisty and cunning as anything that runs on four legs. He will be up one hedge and down another, across the corner of a field, along the top of a wall, into a hole and out again the other side, up a tree, and Lord knows where, in the course of a short run, while at other times he will go clear away like a travelling fox, heading for home, though taking full advantage of cover all the time.

In order to eject him from holes when he goes to ground, one generally carries a few squibs or lengths constructed hutch for them with two compartments, one closed for sleeping, and the other open with a removable bottom tray.

Absolute cleanliness must be insisted on, not just a clean up once a week, but a thorough cleaning-out and removal of all filth and old food every day. Failure to observe this rule leads sooner or later to footrot and other evils. Some dry straw or shavings, enough to make a thick bed, should be provided, and frequently changed.

As to feeding, most people favour a staple diet of bread and milk for ferrets, and probably this is as good as anything, provided that old, sour food is not left in the pans, and that the latter are scalded out daily. A certain amount of freshly killed animal food is also necessary, and may be supplied in the shape of sparrows, rats, mice, chickens' heads, etc., or lean meat of any kind.

The last ferrets which I had were fed entirely on raw meat and fresh water, no food of any other description being given, and they were always in perfect health and condition.

The female ferret, before she produces her young, must have a hutch to herself and the young, and must not be touched for a month, else she will eat them.

- Ferrets for ratting should be of small size, and preferably bred from ratting strains, such as are kept by professional rat-catchers. It is not every ferret that is a good ratter, by any means. Ferrets that have been used exclusively for rabbiting may get badly bitten, and even killed, if suddenly introduced into a colony of big rats, and it is essential that they should have some preliminary training in the art of rat fighting before tackling a job of this kind. A beginning should be made with small holes, or even by putting the ferret into a barrel with one or two medium-sized rats and letting him kill them. Ratting ferrets must never on any account be muzzled, nor should they be encumbered with belts or other paraphernalia.

Liners cannot be used for ratting.

When ratting with ferrets I would never have more than two dogs working at one time. A lot of dogs leads to confusion and bother. It is also desirable that one of the dogs should be an old experienced hand at the work, and be " true to hole "—*i.e.*, capable of saying at once whether a hole is inhabited or not. Dogs that scratch at any old hole are a nuisance, and waste much valuable time.

As to localities, almost any place that holds rats may be ferreted, and the method of dealing with them is much the same everywhere. First let the dogs hunt round and find an occupied hole, trusting, of course, to your old dog till the young one has proved himself ; then take up both the dogs and make them stand three feet clear, either behind or on one side of the hole (not in front of it). Next put in your ferret and stand clear yourself. The ferret may be some time away if the place is a big one, but the dogs must remain absolutely still and quiet all the time. When a rat bolts it is instantly seized and killed by the dogs, who must be taught to drop the carcase at once, and return to their place to wait for the next one.

The whole art really lies in training the dogs to remain absolutely still, without whining, in the place you put them, and to kill and drop the rat at once. All young dogs, and indeed some old ones, will want to carry the rat about and shake it long after it is dead, but this must be severely discouraged.

Some ferrets, if they happen on a nest of nice, juicy young rats, are apt to lie up for a sleep after enjoying their meal, and nothing is more trying to the temper of the rat-catcher, particularly if the locality does not permit of digging. The best means I know of for dealing with this nuisance is to carry a few short lengths— say, four inches—of Bickford's fuse in your pockets, light one of them with a fusee, and shove it into the hole, and you may expect to see Mr. Ferret come out at a run. Of course, great care must be exercised in

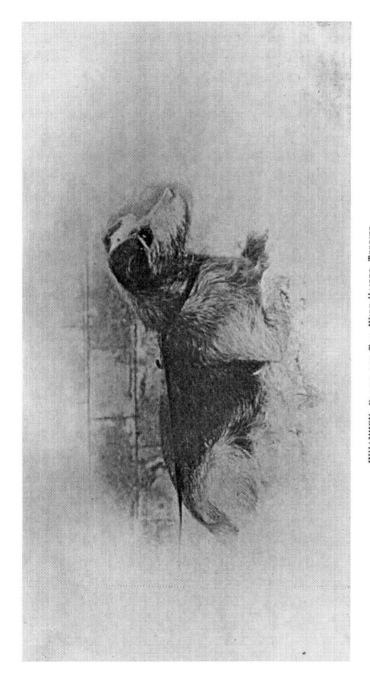

WHANKEY, BLACK-AND-TAN WIRE-HAIRED TERRIER.

using fuses in the neighbourhood of buildings or anywhere else where there is danger of starting a fire.

Sometimes, if the hole be a short one, blowing tobacco smoke into it will bring out a ferret.

Ratting without ferrets, though not nearly so prolific of results, is much better hunting than the former method, and permits of the employment of any number of dogs.

The implements necessary are a small ferreting spade and a light crowbar or pointed iron rod of the length and thickness of a walking-stick, the top being forged with a loop or crook to form a handle.

The method of hunting is simple and obvious. You work along the hedges, ditches, old banks, or any other place where rats do hide, the dogs hunting around and testing every hole. When they discover one which is tenanted they will commence barking, scratching and tearing up the earth with their teeth to get at the inmates, but will not often succeed in doing so without assistance from the master. Sometimes, if you can keep all the dogs away from the hole for a little while, you can get the rat to bolt by driving your bar into the ground where you suppose the end of the hole is, and working it about. Rats seem to hate the noise of iron grating on stones, but, of course, even that will not force them to bolt into the jaws of a pack of Terriers. If the bar fails, the spade must be brought into play, but only to help the dogs from time to time. Let them do most of the work themselves.

In a great many places one can do very little digging for fear of damaging property, such as walls, fences, etc., and if you are working without ferrets there is nothing for it then but the sulphur bellows, a little-known but most efficient apparatus when properly used, as it will not alone clear rats out of holes, but will drive them from behind unmovable pieces of furniture and fixtures, such as bins, mangers, etc.

The outfit, which is sufficiently simple and not too expensive, consists of a bellows or large air-pump, attached to which is a container to hold the fumigant, the latter being fitted with a short flexible hose as an exhaust.

The container is charged with a little live charcoal and chopped straw, or anything else that will smoulder, and sulphur. The exhaust pipe is then shoved into the rat hole, or wherever it is needed, and you pump away. When smoking out holes in banks, etc., you should pack a little turf or earth round the exhaust pipe to keep the smoke from escaping by the same hole it goes in.

This is quite one of the most successful methods of dealing with rats that I know of. Care must be taken, however, not to allow the dogs into the smoke, as it spoils their noses for the rest of the day.

Some bellows have a container fixed at the side so as to inhale the smoke, so to speak, on expansion, and blow it out on compression.

Great fun is often to be had with rats when a stack is being threshed. The number killed is, as a rule, disappointing, and bears no relation to the numbers seen, but the excitement and fun make up for the small-ness of the bag. All dogs, and humans too, are pressed into service for this work, which is not without a spice of danger, for one is always liable to have a dog or a foot transfixed by some fool with a pitchfork, or have a rat run up one's trousers, a truly terrifying experience.

In conclusion, wherever you go ratting, do not leave dead rats lying about. Bury them.

RABBITS.

I have so far purposely avoided any mention of rabbiting, as I do not consider it to be legitimate terrier sport, and also because I hold that if terriers are to be used for stoat and otter hunting, ratting, etc., rabbits must be regarded severely as " riot," and no dog ever permitted to chase one, otherwise you will always have half your pack scratching in rabbit burrows, to the detriment of sport.

TIM, BLACK-AND-TAN WIRE-HAIRED TERRIER.

I do not think it is possible completely to break terriers from chasing fur, but much may be accomplished by firmness, and by never overlooking, much less encouraging, a breach of discipline.

The temptation to take his terriers out with the gun is of course very great for a shooting man, but I venture to think it is bad policy. Of course, there are some old sinners that cannot be spoilt, having been permitted to chase from their early youth. A day with the gun won't hurt such as these, but young dogs are much better left at home, except when needed for legitimate hunting.

Another great objection to using valuable terriers for rabbiting is the danger of their being accidentally shot. Numbers are killed every year in this way by excitable and inexperienced gunners, and even careful shots often cannot avoid accidents in cover, when there are half a dozen or more dogs out.

I have never tried the experiment of rearing young puppies with tame rabbits about the kennel, but I daresay it might be successful in making them steady later on.

WATER HENS.

Water-hen hunting cannot, perhaps, be considered sport of a very high order, but such as it is, it may occasionally afford half an hour's amusement on a dull afternoon, or an excuse for a country walk.

Water hens are amongst the commonest of our inland aquatic birds, and there are few streams, ponds, or watercourses with good cover but harbour a few.

They are pretty little creatures, and add something to the beauty of an English landscape, so one would be sorry to see them exterminated ; but it must be admitted that they are very destructive to trout spawn, which they devour, and to wild ducks' eggs, which they seem to break out of pure malice. Their numbers, therefore, should be kept within bounds.

Water hens have a very strong scent, which all dogs seem to follow with pleasure ; even pointers and setters will point them till broken of the habit.

The hunting of water hens with terriers needs very little description. Taking your little pack down to the waterside, you throw them into cover—reeds, brambles, or whatever it may be—and encourage them to well beat out every hole and corner, for water hens are great skulkers, and often take a lot of shifting. As soon as the dogs find a bird, and get her well on the run, they will bustle her about for a minute or two, when, if she finds that she is being hard pressed, she will take to wing and fly perhaps fifty or one hundred yards up or down stream, or maybe to some neighbouring ditch or hedgerow. The dogs are now, of course, completely at fault, and must be lifted and put on the line again at the new place—*i.e.*, where the water hen was marked down and so on. A water hen's principal way of evading her enemies is by diving and remaining under water, which she can do for a long time, and when obliged to come to the surface for air, will just protrude the top of her bill, and remain perfectly still and invisible, except to a keen and practised eye.

A good water dog with a good nose comes in here, as he will get the scent as it is carried down stream by the water, and will quickly dive and capture his prey.

Water hens, when hunted by dogs, also often take refuge in the tops of the bushes and hedges, and even in high trees ; from such positions they must be dislodged with clods of earth, or any other missile that comes to hand.

Any sort of dogs do for this sport. Spaniels revel in it, though their masters do not always approve, particularly if they are much used on legitimate wild fowl.

If you do much otter hunting it is just as well to leave water hens severely alone, or your pack will be eternally at riot.

CASUALTIES AND FIRST AID.

In badger, fox, and otter hunting, casualties amongst the dogs employed are unfortunately only too common. The hurts received may vary from a few trifling punctures, or a torn ear, to the most ghastly and sometimes fatal injuries.

In view of this a first-aid outfit should always accompany the sportsman who goes in pursuit of dangerous game. This need not be elaborate—just a canvas roll containing a bottle of diluted antiseptic for cleansing wounds, some cotton wool, lint, a bandage or two, and surgical needles and silk.

In dealing with lacerated wounds, such as are usually caused by the bite of a badger or fox, the first thing to do is to thoroughly clean the wound of all impurities with some simple disinfectant, such as Jeyes' Fluid, diluted. The edges of the wound should then be brought together as close as possible, and a pad of lint, soaked in disinfectant, placed over it. Keep the lint in its place with a bandage, if possible. In bad cases stitching must be resorted to. Never cut away any loose bits of skin or tissue, unless it is certain that they are retarding the healing of the wound. You cannot tell whether this is so at the time the wound is received.

Never hesitate to consult a properly qualified vet. if you have any doubts as to the condition of the patient.

Puncture wounds, such as result from simple bites, should be syringed out with an antiseptic, and the external wound kept open by a plug of cotton wool soaked in antiseptic.

Sprains sometimes occur with working terriers ; the muscles most commonly affected are those of the thigh, shoulder, and breast. Bathing with warm water, and rubbing in some good embrocation, such as Elliman's, is an effective treatment.

Injuries to the eye, outside of bathing with warm water and boracic, should always be left to the care of a professional man.

MEDICINES.

A few simple remedies for everyday accidents and ailments should be kept in every kennel, and for these one cannot do better than stick to the preparations of such well-known and reliable firms as Sherley and Spratts, Limited.

A bottle of some good disinfectant is useful for cleaning cuts and wounds, and general washing purposes, of both dogs and kennels.

A bottle of peroxide of hydrogen is invaluable for the treatment of sloughing sores, canker of the ear, etc., etc.

For skin troubles generally, paraffin oil and sulphur mixed is the best local application I know of, and it is also an excellent hair stimulant for bald places.

Worm powders or capsules are in constant demand, and purgative pills of some kind should be kept handy.

Canker cure is a good thing to have by one, though terriers are not so subject to this unpleasant malady as are the larger breeds.

A bottle of Elliman's should be kept for sprains, etc.

For accidents generally you will require lint, cotton wool, bandages, safety pins, oil silk and surgical needles, though when it comes to stitching it is better, if possible, to enlist the services of a veterinary and have the job done properly.

It is a mistake to bandage up every little scratch or cut on a dog. If he can reach the place with his tongue he will, as a rule, effect a more rapid cure by licking the place.

HOUSING.

All sporting dogs are better for being kept in properly constructed kennels, when not at work or exercise. Most of us, however, will not have kennels built as such at our disposal, and must make shift with a stable or outhouse, or even barrels on their side under a shed.

Where only one or two dogs are kept, they often have the run of the house, and sleep in their master's room ; but even these would be better housed apart. A house dog more often than not does not settle to sleep till the last member of the household has retired, and is awake with the earliest riser in the morning, and so does not get as much rest as the dog who is kennelled at 5 or 6 o'clock in the evening, and left there till required next day.

With dogs just kept for pets and companions this is a matter of no consequence, but for dogs who do a hard day's work, it is much better to feed them up and put them to bed as soon as you return from the chase.

With regard to improvising kennels in a stable, wood shed, or any such place, there are two or three points to be considered—

(1) The dogs must not sleep on the ground, but must have a bench or bed raised a foot or so off the floor.

(2) They must have a plentiful supply of clean straw or pine shavings, changed frequently.

(3) The place must be made, as far as possible, rain and draught proof.

With regard to (1), two or three planed deal planks fitted and nailed together, and raised on chocks of wood or bricks, and placed in a corner, will do at a pinch, though a bench fitted to the wall with hinges, so that it can be turned up for cleaning purposes, will make a neater job and be better in every way.

(2) Long straw is the best bedding for dogs, and they much prefer it to anything else ; but failing this, soft pine shavings do very well. Hay is poor bedding, as it soon becomes foul and sodden. Old blankets and rugs, etc., are an abomination, and should never be used if anything else is obtainable.

A piece of board, three or four inches high, may be nailed round the edge of the sleeping bench, to keep the litter in place.

(3) Draughts : All holes and cracks in the walls and doors should be repaired, and the bottoms of the

doors made to fit close to the sill, ventilation being obtained by having a window open at the top.

In hot weather, of course, dogs must have all the air they can get, and windows and doors may then be kept open wide.

Barrels laid on their side in an outhouse make good kennels for terriers, but they are a little more trouble to keep clean. They also should be raised well off the ground, and securely chocked up. A piece of board should be nailed across the bottom part of the mouth of the barrel, to keep the bedding in place.

When selecting barrels for this purpose, choose good, clean, sound ones. Old shaky casks soon become draughty and uncomfortable. Also see that there are no nails or splinters sticking up inside to injure your dog.

A good strong staple may be driven into the side of each barrel, and will be convenient for fastening a chain to when required.

Straw can generally be obtained in small quantities from farms and livery stables, and wood shavings from any wood yard or joiner's shop.

Dogs should at all times have access to drinking water, and both the water and the vessel containing it should be perfectly clean.

—

FOOD.

The feeding of dogs is much more of a problem in these days of high prices than in the days of yore, when meal was cheap, and butchers' offal to be had for the asking. Now, even four or five small terriers may well run one into considerable expense in the way af food.

In large households the scraps left over from the table, if carefully saved, will generally provide a meal for two or three dogs at least, but in small establishments there may not be enough leavings to feed more than one ; the rest must be begged or bought.

If you happen to have any good friends in the hotel or restaurant business, you may perhaps persuade them to put a pailful of scraps on one side for you daily; and as you will probably have to fetch it yourself, a small covered pail is recommended as being less conspicuous in the street.

I am a great believer in working dogs getting plenty of flesh meat, and if you are driven to purchase the same, the cheapest obtainable is generally lights and throttles from the butcher. For the rest, condemned ships' biscuit is sometimes to be had at a low figure, and if only slightly damaged is cheap food ; but rotten, cavilly stuff is dear at any price, and should never be used. Rice and oatmeal are also sometimes obtainable in a slightly damaged condition, and make good porridge for dogs, whilst boiled fish heads, mixed with broken bread or potatoes, are much appreciated.

A certain amount of green food is very desirable, and a little sulphur mixed up with the food, once a week or so, will keep dogs' coats in fine condition.

A stick of sulphur placed in the water pan is quite useless.

Do not feed all the dogs from one dish. Terriers are naturally quarrelsome creatures, and the weaker and slower eating dogs never get their full share. Give each dog his own portion, and stand by yourself to see fair play and no squabbling. If left to themselves, the stronger dogs are apt to wolf their own whack and then have a go at some other fellow's ; they even forget their accustomed chivalry at such times, and are not by any means above driving a bitch away from her dinner and eating it themselves.

Rabbit and chicken bones are better cut out of the menu, but large beef and mutton bones are good, and dogs get a lot of satisfaction out of gnawing them. You cannot prevent dogs taking bones into their beds, but they should be removed next day, and disposed of in some place where they cannot be resurrected.

The Sealyham Terrier as a Sporting Companion.

THERE are few breeds that make a better sporting " pal " than the Sealyham Terrier, and many not nearly so good. He is, in the first place, a " hardy annual," and usually " as game as they make 'em," and withal intelligent and sensible. There is, moreover, no breed better adapted anatomically and physically for underground work in connection with the badger, a very hard-bitten animal, and in the haunts of the otter, which is perhaps a harder-bitten animal still, and a semi-aquatic animal, which can consequently take refuge in and under water, in addition to his subterranean retreats. Sealyham Terriers, as a rule, are good swimmers, their heavy-boned legs, big pads, and rotund bodies serving them well for purposes of water work.

Sealyhams may be trained and used with success upon fox, stoat, weasel, rabbit, rat, and may even be broken to the gun, with, however, somewhat less success, speaking generally. The dog's great fort in the field of sport, and for which he is better adapted than any other dog probably, is in connection with the badger, hunting " Mr. Brock," and taking part in ousting him out of his natural earth, which provides some very bracing and exhilarating sport both for the dog and its human followers.

For purely " badgering " purposes some sportsmen prefer the Sealyham a little crooked in his forelegs, somewhat on the lines of the Dachshund—the German badger dog. The theory of this is that the dog with such foreleg formation is better adapted to scratching the earth away behind him when digging for the badger. But—and it is a big BUT—dogs so formed usually are wide in the brisket, and dogs wide in brisket are usually shallow in chest. Wider the brisket and wider must be the aperture of the earth—and, indeed, the whole burrow—which has to be made in an endeavour to reach the badger ; whereas if the dog's front was comparatively narrow, and his chest deep instead of wide, with short, straight, and stout forelegs, which all Sealyhams

BOWHIT BETTY.

ought to have, he would have ample play for his work of excava-tion and require a smaller burrow, and the displacement of less earth,which presents no disadvantage in the performance of the pursuit of badger digging, but, on the other hand, every advantage.

The following are the Rules formulated by the Sealyham Terrier Club for badger-digging trials :—

RULES FOR BADGER-DIGGING TRIALS.

1. That the object of this Committee is to test the efficiency of Sealyham and other working Terriers in natural earths.

2. That the names of any dogs required to be tested for certificates must be sent to the Secretary not later than the Saturday night previous to the Dig.

3. That there shall be Club Digs on the second and fourth Thursday of each month, from May in one year to the end of December in the following year.

4. All dogs must be at the place selected for the digs not later than 11 o'clock on the morning of the date fixed.

5. All dogs to be chained up a sufficient distance from the earth, so as not to interfere or hamper the competing Terriers, and no other dogs shall be permitted near the earth while the trials are in progress.

6. All digging arrangements to be left entirely to the duly appointed officials, and no interference will be permitted on any pretence whatsoever.

7. No dog to be put to ground until the owner receives notice from the judges that they are ready.

8. No persons except the judges, officials, and diggers, and the person working his or her dog, to be allowed near the earth.

9. All dogs to be given a reasonable time to enter, and if at the expiration of that time they decline to work, the judges can order that they shall be taken up and the next dog shall be called for.

10. There shall be one or more Club judges officiating at all Trials, it being understood that no dog owned or otherwise connected with a judge shall be presented for trial on the day he officiates as judge at such trial.

11. That 1s. Entry Fee will be charged for each dog presented for trial, such fee to be applied towards the expenses incurred in connection with the trial.

12. That not more than ten or less than six dogs shall compete at each trial unless the judge rules otherwise.

13. That all uncertificated dogs shall have preference over those holding certificates.

14. Should there be an insufficient number of dogs entered for a par-ticular Trial the Secretary shall have power to notify the owners, and hold the entries over until the next dig.

15. A non-member of the Sealyham Terrier Club or Working Terrier Club shall not, whether working his or any other person's dogs, interfere in any way.

16. The decision of the judges shall in all cases be final, and any person or member adversely criticising the action of the judges shall have his name brought before the General Committee, who may penalise him by withholding the certificate.

17. The Committee beg to ask that all members will preserve badgers, and not frequent the earths with dogs where the Club digs are to take place.

18. Only dogs entered for competition will be allowed to be present at the Trials.

These Rules are subject to alterations and additions.

The best treatise on "badgering," in respect of its proper and practical prosecution, appears in the little book, "Terriers for Sport," by Pierce O'Conor, which every sporting-terrier enthusiast should have in his possession. We therefore reproduce that portion of Mr. O'Conor's article on badger digging, which is as follows :—

BADGER DIGGING.
PERSONNEL AND EQUIPMENT.

Three things are above all necessary to success in badger digging—good dogs, good diggers, and a good ear. Add to these a good slice of patience and a capacity for suffering disappointment without becoming unduly discouraged, and you have it all.

I have already remarked on the importance of having hard, well-entered dogs. With dogs that come out of the earth every half-hour, you may as well go home, for you will never handle a badger in a week, except by demolishing the whole earth, in which case that locality is lost to you for sport in the future. No fox or badger will go there again for many a long day, if ever.

Next to good dogs come good diggers. Lazy, idle fellows, or bad workmen who don't know their business, spoil many a promising hunt.

Except in very large, difficult places, where it may be necessary to sink two, or even three, trenches, or where the work is so extensive as to require relays of diggers, two or three good men will do all you want. But they must be keen, and have a real taste for the work.

The late war afforded excellent practice in trench digging to some of us, and many old soldiers are first-rate hands with the pick and shovel ; they are generally good sportsmen, too.

The idle loafer picked up outside the village pub. is, as a rule, useless, and spends most of his time mopping his brow and trying to get a pull at the beer-jar ; and, talking of beer, it is well to make a hard-and-fast rule that refreshment is only for those who earn it, and not for spectators.

With some Terrier clubs it is the custom to take round a "cap" after the dig, to pay the diggers and meet other casual expenses. One should have an understanding with the diggers that they are to be paid so much per day (or half a day, as the case may be), with a bonus for every full-grown beast taken, or else to divide the cap money, less a percentage. Personally,

LITTER BY HAMPTONIA TARTAR.

I much prefer the former plan, but much depends on the class of men with whom you have to deal.

Finally, a good ear is important, that you may readily ascertain the exact spot below which the dog and badger are situated, and so commence your digging operations in the right place. Nothing is more discouraging to men than to find, after half an hour's work on a hot day, that their labour has been in vain, and a fresh start has to be made somewhere else.

EQUIPMENT.

With regard to the question of equipment generally, this should be kept as simple as possible ; a multitude of fancy tools and appliances is very inconvenient to transport, and generally unnecessary.

A couple of spades, a pick or two with adze-shaped heads (such as are known as " twobills " or " diggers " in some parts of the country), a crowbar, a shovel, a chopper or hatchet for cutting roots, and badger tongs are the essentials. There are also one or two little special tools known as spuds and scrapers, which are useful in small places. A stout canvas sack, ventilated with brass eyelet holes, and having a draw-string and strap and buckle at the neck, is also required to put your quarry in when captured.

THE DIG.

Being now fully equipped with the necessary dogs and tools, and attended by a couple of good spade men, we may take the field. The first thing to do, having acquired information as to the position of the earths you mean to work, is to make a thorough inspection of the ground, ascertain what openings there are, and whether they have been recently used, and by what animals. The earth will commonly be situated on the side of a hill, with entrances above and below, and some men hold that the dog should always be put in at the lower hole, while others favour that on the higher ground. There is really nothing whatever in it ; it is purely a matter of chance. Just loose your best and most reliable dog and leave matters to him, and he will soon decide for himself which passage will lead him most quickly to his foe. If the earth is unoccupied a good dog will lose no time in letting you see that such is the case, for he will leave the earth altogether and go hunting for a better place.

If, on the other hand, your dog goes to ground and remains there, listen attentively at the mouth of the hole for the first sounds of combat, and then cheer your dog on with all the power of your lungs. After a few minutes you may expect a period of silence, and then the fight will commence anew in some other part of the earth. If the place is a big one you may now slip another dog to assist, but not if there is a likelihood of the dogs fighting each other. A dog and bitch are best suited for this job, as there is then no danger of a row. After two or three sparring matches and running fights things will probably settle down below, and then, with your ear to the ground or against a crowbar driven in, you must endeavour to arrive at the spot immediately above the fight, and commence digging.

As has been indicated in a previous chapter, it is not always easy to know at first sight what animal you have got to deal with in an earth, whether fox or badger ; the external evidences are not invariably unmistakable, but when you know your dogs their manner of working will generally not leave you long in doubt.

Having engaged in two or three lively duels with the dogs in different chambers and passages, the badger as a rule sets up pretty quickly, and the continuous baying of the Terriers in one place leaves little doubt as to where digging operations must begin. With a fox the procedure will be much the same where the earth is small, but in a big working, where he has lots of room, things are somewhat different. After the first sounds of warfare, which will only last a few minutes, there will be a rush and a scuffle, and then silence. After a while out will come your dog in great excitement, nose down, convinced that his adversary has given him the slip and gone away, but almost immediately back he will go, and after a few more minutes' exploring you will hear him find his fox afresh and recommence the fight. You now start digging, but at the first few strokes of the pick off goes Reynard again, and it may be an hour, with two or three dogs after him, before he is finally cornered.

Another useful test in cases of uncertainty is the examination of the dog's claws as soon as he shows up; there will often be found the hairs of the hunted animal sticking to them. Fox fur particularly clings tenaciously to a dog's feet, and the odour of fox is also sometimes quite noticeable about his mouth.

When baying a badger most dogs give tongue more continuously than when dealing with a fox. With the latter animal their inclination seems to be to close with their adversary and to bring matters to a head as soon as possible. One can still hear the fight going on, of course, but not a succession of barks—rather a muffled sound of fierce and bloody combat, and no sparring.

In hunting a fox underground care must be taken to stop all holes but one, and have that well watched, otherwise he will surely bolt when you least expect it; but with a badger these precautions are usually omitted, for a badger seldom bolts, but fights it out to the bitter end, or if he does mean to take to the country he usually does so as soon as the dog is put in and before digging operations are started.

At a recent meet of the Bideford Badger Club a badger was twice bolted from two different earths without a spade being put to the ground, and gave an excellent run of an hour or so, with all the Terriers and the whole field after him, before he was finally lost.

Before commencing digging it is most important to form an opinion as to the direction of the line of the passage or gallery in which your dog is, so that you may sink your trench at right angles to it. You will thus make sure of cutting the gallery somewhere, otherwise you may be excavating in a direction parallel to it, and put in a lot of useless work before you find your mistake.

Always insist on your men cutting a good wide trench while they are about it, and see that they maintain the width as they go down; there is nothing more annoying than to see men poking about in the bottom of a narrow trench, with no room to use their tools. It is in these little details that the keen and experienced digger evidences his value; he knows his job and understands what you are trying to do, while the casual labourer is just working for his pay, and is more or less in the dark as to what is really required of him.

As the work goes on, and you are getting nearer the scene of combat, caution your men to go carefully with their picks, lest they suddenly come upon the dogs and injure them.

The din of battle becomes louder and clearer every minute, and then perhaps there will be a horrid noise of a dog in agony, and one of your gallant little warriors will appear at the mouth of the hole badly torn and mauled. He should be immediately taken up, put on a lead, and his wounds washed and dressed, while another dog is despatched to take his place at the front.

The diggers will now be working fast and furious, and louder and clearer sounds the baying of the dogs. Presently a stroke of the spade lays bare the passage where the fight is in progress, and if you are lucky you may be close enough to handle your beast without more ado. If, however, dogs and badger are still out of reach, stop any other holes leading into the trench, open up the gallery till you can get your tongs to bear, and drag the badger out, dogs and all. See that your sack is held ready, and after the dogs have been taken up, pop him in. A sacked badger should not be left on the ground, or he will tear his way out of the bag. The bag should rather be suspended to the branch of a tree if it has to be left for any time.

If dogs and badger are, say, ten or twelve feet from the trench, when you reach the gallery, it is best to get the dogs out if possible. Clear everybody away from the trench, and enjoin silence. Then commence digging right over the place where the badger is. Having no dog to contend with, and hearing the digging going on above him, the badger will generally bolt into the trench himself, where he must be seized before he has time to get back. Sometimes you may lose your badger at the last moment, so to speak, through his digging his way through into some neighbouring gallery, and making his escape.

Badgers are also very prone, if they get a chance, to earth themselves in—that is, they throw up a solid wall of earth behind them, and between themselves and the dog, blinding the latter, and completely blocking the passage, and then adding to the thickness of this as they go along. Hard-bitten, experienced dogs seldom allow time for this operation on the part of Master Brock, but with young dogs, or those not so hard, this trick sometimes succeeds, and delays matters considerably, as even a good dog going down after may have considerable difficulty in fresh finding his badger through a three-foot wall of earth.

Sometimes badgers are already earthed in when one arrives at the scene of operations (probably having been scared by some dog or person just before), and then it takes a good dog to get on terms with them. Occasionally a badger will dig himself out of the earth altogether and take to the country, but this happens but rarely.

Always be careful to fill in your trenches, and make good any damage before leaving the earth. Foxes and badgers will not resort to a place that has been left in ruins; and remember that it is only by courtesy of the owner or occupier of land that one hunts at all, so that anything that is likely to cause him loss or annoyance must be avoided.

BADGER HUNTING AT NIGHT.

This is a branch of the sport which is very little practised, and for good reason, for it entails being abroad at most unconscionable hours of the night, and stumbling and falling about in the dark, to say nothing of frightening cattle and sheep, etc.

Indeed, unless there are badgers close to where you live or are staying with your dogs, the game is hardly worth the candle.

The procedure, which is simple, is as follows :—

On a fine night, with a good moon, a careful and, if possible, experienced watcher secretes himself just before dark in some place where he can obtain a clear view of the earth and down wind of it.   He must be very patient, for he may have a long and dreary vigil, and he must never for one instant take his eyes off the mouth of the hole.   If he does, that will be just the time that Master Brock chooses to slip out unobserved.

Badgers are extraordinarily cautious and suspicious creatures, and never leave their earth without waiting for some considerable time at the entrance, listening and sniffing the wind to detect the presence of an enemy.   The snapping of a twig or the rustle of a leaf at this time is sufficient to put them down for the rest of the evening.   Even after coming out, they will often remain playing about outside for some considerable time before they set forth on their nightly prowl, and will be ready to pop back again at the first sight or sound of danger.

If and when the observer sees the badgers emerge from their dwelling, and disappear into the woods, he gives them twenty minutes' law so that they may get well away, and then fastens a sack or large purse net in the mouth of the hole, pegging it lightly down, and fastens the draw-string to a stump or tree.   Having done this he stops any holes which are not bagged, with strong faggots previously prepared, and signals the huntsman by whistle or flashlight that all is ready.

The Master then unkennels his dogs, and draws round in a wide circle until he hits the trail of the badgers.   As soon as the dogs settle on the line and commence to give tongue, the badgers realise that all is not well, and make for home at their best pace, the hunt stumbling along behind as best they can.

If Brock is being pressed pretty closely, he will generally dash straight into the sack on arrival at the earth, but if he has time to investigate, he may scent danger, and give it the go-by.   For this reason it is well for the watcher to remain on guard, and when he sees the badger approaching the earth he should show himself and yell.   This will generally have the effect of hastening matters, and leave Master Brock no time for thought. As soon as the badger is bagged, the watcher runs in and makes all secure, the hunt comes up, and all is over but the final whoo-hoop !

One can, of course, dispense with the services of a watcher, if need be, but in that case one must not bag the earth or commence to draw before eleven o'clock or midnight, and even then you cannot be sure that your badger has gone away, and may spend half the night hunting for nothing.

No earth stopping must be done at any of the entrances to the sett before the badger comes out.   All preparations, moreover, should be made the previous day, and no one should be allowed near the earth on the day of the hunt, for if he hears people moving about over his head Brocky will remain at home, and so may you for all the sport you will get.

The sport of badger hunting is one that has grown considerably in late years, the advent and growing popularity of the Sealyham Terrier having given it a great fillip.   And " badgering " is a form of sport indulged in by all classes of the community from the nobility down to the artisan, the former dropping their class

Capt. Jocelyn Lucas Putting a Sealyham in a Badger Hole.

distinction in order to mingle among the more humble of their fellows in the pursuit of a sport in which all have a common interest, and whose aspirations are identical.

Badger digs in all parts of England and Wales (and occasionally in Scotland) are now quite a common occurrence, and attract a lot of enthusiastic followers along the country-side where they take place.

The following, beginning with the late Capt. John Edwardes, and including the late Mr. C. J. Gladdish Hulkes, J.P., were and are among the more prominent zealots who have associated them-selves with it, and who at present indulge in the sport :—

Lord Kensington, Capt. J. H. Howell, M.F.H. ; Mr. Fred. W. Lewis, J.P. ; Major Harry Jones, Major David Davies, M.P. ; Capt. Jocelyn Lucas, M.C. ; Capt. Checkland Williams, Mr. H. B. Gwyther, Mr. Sid Bowler, Mr. Geo. Scott Mansfield, Mr. H. Ridley, and many others.

Symptoms and Treatment of Common Ailments.

IN treating upon the various diseases to which dogflesh is heir it is not my intention, in the scope of this little work, to go deeply into the same, and this from a scientific point of view, which it would be impossible for me to do, since I am not a qualified veterinary surgeon.

I must content myself, therefore, by enumerating the more common ailments and diseases of the dog, and giving advice, as the result of my half-century's experience in the breeding and exhibition of dogs, and simple remedies which I have found efficacious in their treatment, before the ailment or disease has got beyond the power of a lay-owner to arrest or cure. When this state of things happens it is best to call in a qualified vet. without further delay, so that he may have a chance of treating the dog before it has gone too far.

A deeper insight into the ailments and diseases of the dog and their treatment on more scientific lines will be found in the little book entitled " Everyday Ailments of and Accidents to the Dog," published by *Our Dogs* at 4s. 9d. post free, from which some of my remedies are taken.

WORMS.—These pests are among the first to attack the dog, and are often imbibed by the infant with its mother's milk. This shows how necessary it is before breeding from a bitch to make sure that she is free from worms, and the same with the stud dogs, for worms are hereditary. There are three kinds of worms—viz., long tape worms, round wire-like worms, and small seat worms. The last-named are of little consequence. Tape worms, of which there are several species, are most common in dogs.

Treatment.—Withhold food for 24 hours, then give the dog a dose composed as follows :—

Ethereal Extract of Male Fern..........	10 to 30 drops.
Syrup of Orange......................	1 oz.

[By the courtesy of Capt. Jocelyn Lucas].

CAPT. LUCAS TONGING A BADGER.

For round worms, which are also fairly common, treat, after fasting for 24 hours, by giving the following, viz. :—

R Santonin .... 2 to 10 grains.
Infusia of Quassia .... ½ teaspoonful.

In case of puppies suckling at the breast, half the foregoing quantities should be given, and the dam treated at the same time with the full dose.

There are several ready-made worm specifics for dogs advertised in *Our Dogs*, and sold, one of the best of which for young puppies is " Ruby."

DECAYING TEETH.—The teeth of a dog are very important, and great care should be taken to see that the moment decay is noticeable they are attended to, since the teeth, if neglected, often lead to ulcerated lips, warts on the tongue, etc., etc. Where the teeth are very bad, they are better removed, and where puppies do not cast their first set as the new ones make their appearance, the old ones should be removed.

EAR CANKER,—This is often the result of the dog getting wet frequently and remaining so. The inside of the ears should be well washed with soap and warm water containing a solution of Condy's or Jeyes' Fluids, and when perfectly dry the affected parts should be dressed with a little nitrate-of-silver solution.

MANGE.—There are several forms of mange and skin disease, the most obstinate of cure being follicular mange, which causes the skin to become inflamed and form itself in ridges, which are thrown up by reason of the parasite settling in the "follicles." It is not so contagious as red mange. The following is a good prescription :—

R Liquor Soda .... 1oz.
Creosote .... ½oz.
Methylated Spirit of Wine .... 3½oz.
Almond Oil .... 3½oz.

Mix and dress the affected parts daily.

Eczema is a common form of skin disease, and, too, is difficult to eradicate. The following recipes will be found efficacious :—

Pills, made up as follows :—

R Sulphate of Quinine .... 48 grains.
Arsenious Acid .... 1 grain.
Extract of Taraxacum .... 24 grains.
Confection of Roses......A sufficiency to make 48 pills.

Directions.—Give one pill night and morning, continuing for three weeks at a stretch.

Mixture for Eczema :—

R Liquor Arsenicalis	80 drops.
Tincture of Calumba......................	1oz.
Acetate of Potash	1oz.
Ammoniated Citrate of Iron	1 drachm.
Infusion of Quassia............Add to make 8oz.	

Mix and give one teaspoonful twice daily. and continue for three weeks. Allow a couple of days' respite and then renew the physic for another three weeks. Red mange is also a common form of skin disease which the following ointment will often cure :—

R Oil of Tar.................................	1 drachm
Oleate of Mercury Ointment................	½oz.
Precipitated Sulphur	2 drachms.
Powdered Oxide of Zinc	2 drachms.
Glycerine	1½ drachm.
Soft Soap.................................	2oz.

Mix and apply night and morning.

The various forms of mange are often hereditary, and therefore very difficult of cure. In applying either ointment or liquid dressings, if the hair is on the affected parts, it should be cut off so as to give the application a better chance of getting into the skin.

Dogs suffering from any form of skin disease should be fed largely, if not wholly, on raw, lean fresh meat and butcher's uncleaned offal.

DISTEMPER.—This is probably the most fatal of all the innumerable diseases of the dog, carrying off hosts of the flowers of the breeder's effort annually. It is so disastrous among pedigree dogs that many owners, owing to its highly contagious nature, contend that the disease should be scheduled by the Government in the Contagious Diseases (Animals) Act. The symptoms of the disease are usually very apparent, in the dog becoming quieter and giving up his own voluntary gambols with other dogs, or gallops on his own, remaining in his kennel and seeking isolated quietude. He will also go off his food and drink a lot of water, which is an indication of inflammation having set in. The next thing will be seen a running at the eyes and nose, or both, followed by the eye-balls becoming red and sunken. A cough may or may not accompany the development of the disease. In the case of valuable dogs, when one has acquired this disease, he should be isolated at once, and a qualified veterinary surgeon called in, for preference one who has made a special study of canine

[By the courtesy of Capt. Jocelyn Lucas].

CAPT. LUCAS' TEAM OF SEALYHAMS DRAWING THE RIVER WREAK FOR AN OTTER, WHICH THEY KILLED AFTER A LONG HUNT.

(The pack consisted of 12 couples of bitches and 1 couple of dogs. Two couples came from the stoat-hunting pack of the late Mr. C. J. Gladdish Hulkes.)

pathology and has treated the disease frequently. Why I advise this is because the disease is so doubtful of cure by home and probably unscientific treatment. Besides, it is often accompanied by complications, and if these take an inward form the difficulty of cure is heightened. In the meantime, besides isolation, the dog should be installed in a warm kennel, the temperature of which should never be less than 70° F., and which should be thoroughly disinfected. The dog's eyes and nose should be kept clean continually, and he should be fed on liquid food, such as beef tea, raw fresh eggs beaten up in milk, and raw, lean, fresh meat minced, if he will take it. The following medicine, as a preliminary, may be given twice daily :—

Rectified Spirit of Wine	2oz.
Tincture of Capsicum.....................	½oz.
Bicarbonate of Potash	½oz.
Concentrated Acetate of Ammonia	3 drachms.
Ipecacuanha Wine	½oz.
Chloroform Water	4½oz.

Mix, and give from one teaspoonful to one tablespoonful.

The foregoing is really in the nature of first-aid treatment, and if improvement is not shown in a very short time a veterinary surgeon should be called in for safety, on the principle that " a stitch in time saves nine."

The Hunt Terrier Man and His Dogs

by Fred F. Wood

A MEET of the local pack of foxhounds is always a big event in country villages, everyone seems to turn up, rich and poor, sporting and non-sporting, must come to see the hounds and horses, all so well set off by the scarlet coats, white breeches and velvet caps of the hunt-servants.

There is also another attendant to the pack, the terrier man, he may be a somebody or a nobody so far as the public are concerned. He may be a man of middle age, wearing a dirty purple coat (once scarlet) begged from the kennels, his head, leg and foot-gear may be anything, or he may be a man of independent means whose hobby is following hounds on his own feet and taking with him his own little working terriers. Whatever his station in life may be, to the onlookers he is 'only' the terrier man, but do they realise, that whoever he may be or whatever his station in life, he is a real sportsman or he would not be doing this work, for it is not easy and can be very uncomfortable work. He may frequently have to run or walk as much as twenty miles in a day following hounds, after walking to the meet, and more miles to walk home, sometimes in drenching rain and this may be after an hour or more of hard digging among roots and brambles, if it be necessary to dig out a fox that has been giving trouble among lambs or poultry. This type of fox must be killed or that great friend to hunting, the farmer, will not be quite happy about it.

Then look at his little companions, maybe a couple or a couple and a half of terriers, not much to look at perhaps, the show terrier man might call them ugly little mongrels, but there is no mongrel about them, many of their pedigrees have been as carefully kept as those of the hounds, not for their appearance, but for their qualities. They have to be constructed of bone, wire, and whip cord, and have coats that will keep out cold and wet and then on top of that be as brave as lions, if they are to do the work they are called upon to do. Many people would not like to be in the room with a fox, where there was ample room to get about, so think of those little terriers, they have to creep and squeeze down a long dark hole, where at any moment a fox as large or larger than themselves, may rush and nip them through nose or foot. But are they frightened? no, do they back out? no —they will stay and fight their fox until he bolts or they are dug out, that requires pluck.

What I have written is not taken from books or from what I have been told, it is from my own personal experience, as I have followed hounds on foot for over fifty years and for the latter half of that time had my terriers with me. I could fill a book with experiences and histories of my terriers. I will give only two experiences and one might style them the good and the bad of it.

I walked five miles over the Downs to the meet, with me a little terrier bitch about twelve pounds in weight, we followed hounds up to 2.30 p.m., when they put a fox to ground in a disused badger set. I put the terrier in (at the request of the Master, of course); in half an hour she had bolted two foxes, with very little damage to herself. In half an hour hounds marked a fox to ground in another earth. I put the terrier in again and soon heard a rare battle going on, we soon dug up to her and got her out, badly bitten all over, as there were three foxes in a kind of den where they had room to turn. Before we had finished digging the wind blew up and rain came down in torrents, I had four miles to walk home with a badly damaged terrier tucked inside my coat; before I had covered a quarter of my homeward journey the water was running in at my neck and out at my boots The other day was when the weather was almost like summer and one could sit happily about on the heather. I only had the five mile walk over the Downs to the meet, and then strolled about from point to point; as there was practically no scent and hounds only dodged from one patch of gorse to another, they eventually ran a fox to ground in a short rabbit hole. I had a terrier dog with me I put him in and in ten minutes I had the fox in my hands, it turned out to be a vixen, hounds were taken away arid I put her down to go her own way off.

This was the easy day, with an easy dig and not more than fourteen or fifteen miles covered all day.

Cairns are Working Terriers

We Should Always Keep in View What Was and Is the Proper Job of This Breed

By C. Brewster MacPherson

My knowledge of the Highland terrier as a worker goes back some fifty years, although for many years before that he was used by the hillmen in their pursuit of the fox and otter. Professional foxhunters were to be found all over the Highlands, who kept packs of these hardy dogs and who moved about their district in the fox-hunting season, getting free bed and board at the Moorland farms. A nondescript hound or two often went with the pack whose job it was to beat the woods, driving the outlying fox up to the guns, posted above, or to ground in cairn or moss hole, where the terriers either bolted him to be shot or killed him inside. The type of terrier varied considerably, but they were all alike in their indomitable courage, hardiness and endurance.

In my own district I knew them all, and many a day and night have I spent with them at their job, and often had occasion to admire the pluck and hardihood of these great-hearted little fighters.

Many had ears erect. As many, or more, had them half set, like a deer-hound, which I thought lent an alert and "all there" aspect to their battle-scarred visages. Their jackets were nearly all very hard and short, very deep and dense, with an undercoat, and they were generally larger and more on the leg than those seen on the bench today.

An active, able dog, that could travel through rank heather and get quickly about rocks, being essential in their trade.

A silky topknot-or its constant accompaniment, a soft coat-was in great disfavor, the former always leading to the remark: "there is some cross in him," although many of such were as game as their fellows.

It may be of interest if I described a typical day's hunting of my youth. The date, let us say, was soon after daylight, about April 30.

I would be anxiously awaiting at the trysting place the arrival of the Brocaire fox-hunter and his pack, who soon appeared with two neighboring farmers and a sporting young sheep-farmer, all with guns and followed by a couple of strong hounds and four couples terriers, on couples, except old Fraochan, which always ran loose.

A great dog this, which I have never got out of my mind's vision! A strong terrier about 15 pounds weight, yet active and narrow enough in front; ears half set, and powerful jaw. His jacket a sort of badger color and as hard as cocoanut matting with a gray, grizzled muzzle.

The surest finder in the pack and hero of 100 fights; a Froachan was dear to the heart of "Seumas Bann" -- Fair James -- a tall, handsome fellow, active as a deer, despite his 50 years, a great ally of mine and fox-hunter of all that district.

In action, Fraochan formed Seumas' reserve, and when, at some deep and difficult den, Morag, Teenack, Doran, and many another came out with bloody nose or torn cheek, to confess defeat by some old dog fox, which, getting into a place of vantage, had held off all attack, Seumas would say "Leag, Fraochan"-let go, Fraochan- and Fraochan, unloosed from the walking-stick beside which he had lain curled up, as if fighting was the last thing he was out for, would walk slowly to the hole, shake himself like a ferret, and as slowly disappear with hackles up on his shaggy back.

A few growls faintly heard in the distance, and suddenly the cairn is alive with the din of battle, while Seumas, his head as far in as he could get it, encourages his favorite to deeds of blood. Fraochan, the old warrior was a crafty fighter, and always feinted for his hold, like a boxer for his knockout. And, though I knew him seldom to get badly punished, he would change his grip like lightning from the side of the head to the throat, after which, save for a muffled sound of worrying, silence would reign within.

Moss hole there the terriers were soon at it. Quickly the guns get back into positions commanding the exits and before long the vixen is forced out and duly shot.

After that the cubs are killed inside, old Morag bringing out one for us to see-as she always did-but never more than one.

A great palaver then followed, and it was decided to watch out the night for the fox dog. Luckily it was dry and not extra cold, and oatcakes, cheese and whiskey having been partaken of, we got into sheltered holes and watched.

He did not come at nightfall. But at dawn one of the keepers got a view of his head over a ridge, with a grouse in his mouth, and made an end of him.

Such is the account of a successful hunt when all went well and weather was good. There is another side to the picture when tragedy takes a hand, for it is a hazardous game these little terriers play. Often, too often, when one has descended into the dark ways where "danger roofs the narrow walks of death," it is "seen again no more of man," having, in a cairn, got jammed between two rocks or, in a moss hole, fallen into some deep water hole with steep sides and perished there from drowning.

I once had a terrier; left in a cairn, crawl home on the ninth day a living skeleton. Fortunately, it survived. The head stalker at Achnacarry assured me he lost seven terriers in one season.

The terrier, too, must needs endure great hardship from weather. The Glenmazeran foxhunter, Fraser, having heard of a "den," very deep in the Monaliath, once went out with a few of his terriers. It was a bitter April day and the wet moss "den," very deep and intricate, was very well known to me. The terriers, having done their job, came out, heated by the fight and soaked to the skin in peaty water, to meet the snow and sleet driven on a cruel northeaster.

Fraser, fearing trouble, started for home, taking one little favorite cubbing bitch "in my shirt next my bosom." He had difficulty in getting the others home-"so perished were they with wet and cold"- and, sad to say they all died except the little bitch.

It will be readily understood, therefore, that no terrier not possessed of exceptional strength, courage and hardness, has a chance of standing the hardships which attend their dangerous calling, and that dog of these days differed widely from the great majority of those seen on the bench today.

If any of my readers is in doubt as to what is and what is not a cairn terrier proper, let him wander along the benches at some important show, and ask himself these questions:

"Is any one of this crowd fit to do a 20-mile day over the roughest of country? Fit to face the blinding snows and driving drift and survive the bitter cold of the watch by night? Which of these can I think of as going down into the dark places below and killing there a strong and savage foe? Could fox hunters of old have done their job with such as these?"

If the answer is, as I fear it must be, "No," he will then ask:

"What are all these weak-jawed, silky-haired little atoms-cairns?"

And perchance a gentle voice may answer: "These are the sweetest little pets in the world."

And doubtless they are. But, oh! "Quantum mutates ab ille Hectore."

What I have written is indeed no unfair description of the standardized cairn terriers. There have been a few on the bench, and champions, too, which, in appearance at least, did no discredit to their fighting race. Alas, but how few! They could be counted on the fingers of one hand.

Our inquiring friend, as he moves on, may chance to see one or two strong, hardy customers with murder in their wicked eyes. They have strong, punishing jaws, and are guiltless of Bedlington top knot. Therefore, they are of the "Scottie" type. They are 15 pounds, or mayhap 16 pounds in weight; therefore they are far too large. There is no place for such at shows. Above their despised heads no badge of honor shines. Yet let it not be supposed there is no use for small terriers-all foxhunters used to keep one or two especially for cubs-and they were highly valued.

When the row begins below, the cubs often slip away into small places where the bigger terriers cannot get at them. Then the small terrier, 11 or 12 pounds in weight, has its real value. I always keep several. They are just the small ones of the litters, bred the same, as dauntless in heart and as hard in constitution as their larger brothers, and in no way to regarded as toys.

I have written before frankly of a subject on which I feel strongly. Yet even since the writing I have had cause to hope for a brighter day, and that, like most things bright and fair, comes from the ladies themselves; for by recent posts, I have received letters from several, asking me to test their favorites for working certificates to fox. Moreover, as I write, I have before me a letter from a lady who, after describing adventures of her pack at fox and badger, tells of a sporting otter hunt, where her terriers actually accounted for the quarry which weighed 16 -- pounds, no mean feat.

This is all to the good, and of good omen. "What a woman wills today, God wills tomorrow" -- and may it not be that the terrier of the cairn shall yet, again, come to his won by ways far other than I could have dreamt of it?

To those who would hasten the coming of that day, I would say "keep in view what the terrier's proper job was and is." Breed only from proved workers. Enter them young to small vermin, for this breed, above most require careful entering. Some, indeed, I have known which never "took blood" until after their second year. So if they are, as old Tom Wooton used to say, "bred to murder," don't be in a hurry to draft them, for I have known such to turn out among the best in the end. My own practice is to enter the youngsters, first in the artificial earth to rats and stoats, and when the sterner ordeal of battle comes they have no fear of trusting themselves to the dark deeps below.

There can be no better advice than that of Dandie Dinmont of old who, descriptive of his famous terriers, said: "For it a' depends hoo they are entered ye ken . . . I had them a' regularly entered, first wi rottens, then wi stots and weasels and then wi the tods and brocks and noo they can fear naething that ever cam wi a hairy skin on't."

No description of the working terrier of the Highlands would be complete without some mention of what is, perhaps, the oldest branch of the clan-the Island breed.

In old days, one might see these occasionally among the working packs of the Mainland, where it was named by the hillmen "the old Skye terrier." It was of a very distinctive type, for the most part small -- 11-to-14 lb. dog -- generally dark brindle, or dark gray, the later possessing a grizzled gray muzzle, the ears were erect, the face foxey, the jacket very hard and short with soft close undervest. The sort of coat which if ruffled up with the hand, at once returned to its natural
.

Very game and hardy were they, and much used for bolting the otter from his holt on the rocky shore. Their owners liked them small, their job being not to kill, but to cause the quarry to vacate the premises by incessant harassing tactics. An old dog otter, who has not been hunted outside, will often bolt very readily. I have seen such come out almost as soon as the terrier got out of sight.

This strain of terrier has always claimed my admiration, and I unsuccessfully tried to get them recognized. They are so different from the Mainland type that no doubt it is difficult to get them their due on the bench today. If one appears it is at once turned down as "short of coat," and "wanting in Cairn character."

In truth, they differ so widely that separate classes would have to be provided for them. In appearance, they resemble a neat, small Scottish terrier, and beyond doubt are the parent stock from which the present day "Scottie" has been evolved.

The parrot cry too often heard around the Cairn terrier benches of "Scottie type, horrible visu, away with him," seems indeed to carry with it its own condemnation, when one remembers that such probably shows but a reversion to a type most ancient of all of the terrier family.

I have had the luck to possess several -- two of which I append photographs. I hope to find a dog, but it will prove difficult task to trace out the old strains now. Those of McDonald of Tormore, of the McDonald brothers, of the McKinnons of Kilbride, of "Waternish," have I fear, passed away forever. They were all of the same type as I have described. The pity of it!

It seems certain that, in an evil hour, the Dandie Dinmont cross was introduced in certain strains, hence, doubtless, the topknot so dear to the heart of the showman.

Working Terrier Past and Present

(circa 1907)

by T.F. Dale

reprinted from Blackwood's Edinburgh Mag.
New York Oct. 1907 pp535-541

The man who loves hounds is sure to be interested in terriers. The foxhound and terrier are connected in our minds by their common enmity to the fox.

Indeed, in the warfare against the fox the terrier has been the ally of man for a much longer period then the hound. When stag-hunting was the sport of kings, and before the idea of the fox as a beast of chase had dawned on the nobles and gentry in England and Scotland, the peasants and the terriers were harrying the fox even in his stronghold of Malepartus, as they do to this day in Scotland or Wales, and in the mountain districts of Westmoreland and Cumberland.

It was no doubt in their warfare against vermin that the terriers acquired the characteristics of gameness, hardihood, and intelligence which their successors have inherited. Their evolution has followed the same course as that of all modern breeds of sporting dogs. Chosen at first for working qualities only, it is later refinement which has grafted beauty on to ability. The division of terriers into breeds and their classification at dog-shows is quite a modern development. Terrier was a name give to any hardy, active little dog that would face a badger or a fox in its earth, or sometimes a cat in a corner, the last-named being by no means the least formidable antagonist of the three. There was no exclusiveness in the breeding of a terrier, and he was crossed with the bull-dog to give him courage, with the beagle to improve his nose, and in later days the greyhound to give him speed. The crossing was limited only by the necessities of his work, for the terrier needed to be a comparatively small dog, since a dog over sixteen pounds is too large, and below twelve pounds too small, to be of use for going to ground. I know of course that weight has more to do with make and muscular development than with size, yet nevertheless the weights give a rough method of estimating the limits of serviceable size for the working terrier.

Looking back into the past history of the terrier, I seem to find two different types, which have never the less certain common characteristics. The one an active fairly speedy little dog, with prick ears, and an obvious dash of bull. These were the dogs which in small packs were used to work above ground, and this type well depicted in a beautiful plate, after a painting of Reingale, n the Sportsman's Cabinet (1805), where the terriers are reprinted in the chase foumart, or in the early volumes of the Sporting Magazine, engaged in a most spirited combat with a wild cat. Sharpness, activity, and courage are the characteristics written all over these terriers. Then there were the long low dogs with drop ears, of the type endeared to us by the faithful memories of friends and companions - the Skye, the Dandie Dinmont, the Poltalloch. These were essentially dogs to go to ground, and were protected by their coats from their enemies, while the drop ears were a shield to the auditory organs from falling earth and sand. But if we look closely at these pictures (and the terrier of the late eighteenth and early nineteenth centuries has been fortunate both in his chroniclers and the artist who have painted him), we shall see that they have certain characteristics in common. They are strongly built dogs compact and well knit, with rather short necks and powerful jaws. The modern fox- terrier, with his long graceful neck and narrow snipy jaw, is quite a recent manufacture. The short neck is a great point, since it is necessary for the terrier to be near his work if he is to have full advantage of his immense muscular development of neck, shoulders, and forearms, in conflict with fox and badger.

Then there are the mental characteristics which are common to all terriers: the high-stung nerves, the excitable temperament, a reckless disregard of danger, coupled with (perhaps in part occasioned by) a peculiarly faithful devotion to the chosen master, and I must add, a certain pugnacity. The Skye terrier is in disposition the most typical, for he is a strange hairy bundle of nerves courage, shyness, and intense devotion, so that all dogs I have known it is the Skyes that carried with them, when their short span was ended, a part of my life.

It is interesting to note how highly Scotland was accounted of for its terriers, for of the many old pictures I have studied, nearly all the best dogs were said to come from Scotland.

But of all our dogs there is none so versatile in mind and body as the terrier. There is no service that a dog can do for us in sport or as a companion that he is not capable of. Let us note some examples, old and new, of the many duties which terriers can fulfil.

There lies before me as I write an engraving published in The New Sporting Magazine" for 1833 (p.348). Two terriers, Shivers and Pincher, are depicted listening at a box in which a badger is supposed to be confined. The most notable of the two is "Shivers," described as a Scotch terrier. The portrait is that of a small white dog with a wiry coat, so thick about its neck and shoulders as to be almost like a mane. He has great depth of body, excellent legs and feet, and prick ears, a broad head, and rather a short but very powerful jaw. He was the property of Mr. Surtees, of Hamsterley Hall, Durham, and being described as being the "best dog of the breed in that part of the North of England; and though little, and by no means a heavy animal, there was never a fox or badger found too large or savage for him to grapple and draw. His pluck exceed all belief, and he actually once followed a cat up a chimney, passing over a burning fire in the grate below." The shortness of neck is notable, and its certain that when he had hold of a fox or badger he could use his muscular strength, and that muscular development which is well shown by the artist.

But it is not only the dogs of old times that could draw a fox. When Mr. Chandos Pole was master of the Cattistock, he had a terrier in his kennels of Miss Alys Serrell, of Haddon Lodge (author of 'With Hound and Terrier in the Field"). This dog, named Veto, could draw a fox from any drain. He would go straight up to his fox and close instantly. Thus he took the fox by surprise. He would fix his hold on the side of his head at the end of the jaw. A fox so gripped by a good dog is powerless, and can be easily drawn. Miss Serrell had another dog, Racer, that went with such a dash in a drain that he variably made the fox back out, fighting him face to face to the other end. When Racer was in, the whipper-in would simply wait till the fox's brush appeared and then pull him out.

This is the terrier's legitimate work, but it is difficult to restrain a terrier from attacking any vermin. I knew one terrier in India who devoted herself to the dangerous and exciting sport of snake-killing. Her method was to irritate the snake into sitting up. She would dance round it sparring for an opening as it were. Then with incredible swiftness she darted at the reptile and gripped it close to the head, a sharp bite and the snake was dead. She was marvelously successful, until on an unlucky day, when one of her puppies was with her, she found a snake; the puppy got in her way at a critical moment, and the snake struck Nettle on the nose. The wound was slight, it was cauterized at once, and a strong dose of whiskey was administered. Apparently Nettle was quite well the next morning, but as she was playing with the puppy she suddenly turned head overheels, and when we reached her she was stone dead.

If we looked over the records of past sport we shall find that there is almost nothing terriers have not been used for. There is, in fact, no limit to the sporting uses of the fox terrier. I have one that was an excellent retriever, and in the "The Sporting Magazine" for October 1831 there is a picture of a little wire- haired, prick-eared terrier that is bringing a partridge in its' mouth. I know of two working packs of fox-terriers that hunt rabbits in Dorsetshire, beating the hedgerows and driving the rabbits to the gun. One of these packs, with which I have often been out, is very handy, and the terriers pack well without losing their individuality, What struck me as much as anything is the control they submit. If a terrier has marked a rabbit to ground, he will at once come away from the earth to the whistle, although, as we all know, in the case of less well-broken dogs, a terrier will return again and again to dig at the bury, and, indeed, unless dragged away by force spend half the day there.

In this pack, which has been bred for hunting for many years, there is an interesting example of the inheritance of acquired characteristics, for the dogs bred from those which have been hunting with the pack take to work far more readily than those bought from the outside. Indeed I was watching, only a few days before writing this, the early efforts of a puppy whose father has long been a noted member of the pack. This puppy put his nose down and hunted like a hound, and was never far from the others. On the other hand a bitch from another kennel had an excellent nose, worked hard, faced the briers and thick undergrowth of the Dorsetshire doubles, but was notably independent in her work, constantly being wide of the pack. One Terrier, a leggy black-headed bitch of the modern type, has the curious habit of standing like a pointer when she winds a rabbit lying out in the open. In other respects she works well. I have heard it said that terriers accustomed to work above ground will not go underground to a fox, but this is certainly not the case with these terriers, nor was it so with my own two mentioned elsewhere. Sport to them is sport, whether it is above or below ground, and they always seemed to me to know quite clearly what was expected of them. The pack of terriers

I have mentioned above, until a regular pack of otter-hounds worked the streams in their neighborhood, were able to hunt and kill otters without any assistance from hounds. I may say that the training and discipline of these terriers is carried on without a whip at and. if I may put it so, by an appeal to their intelligence and consideration of their characteristics and dispositions. But their owner feeds them, hunts them, exercises them, and of course enters the puppies so that they have every chance of turning out well.

The best working terriers I have ever owned were Vanity and Vixen. The were given to me when I was stationed at Simla. The latter I gave to a friend, but she was often lent to me on hunting days.

Vanity was a small terrier, very neat and compact, with excellent legs and feet, but rather light and elegant. To look at and in manners she was quite the lady's pet, and altogether the most faithful, affectionate, and intelligent little dog anyone could wish to own. But in spite of her appearances she was game a terrier as I have ever known. At first I only knew she had a marvelous gift for hunting and killing rats, and I recollect a most interesting hunt from the stables at Christchurch Lodge, Simla, with a kill just outside the west door of the church. Circumstances, however, subsequently revealed the full value of my little dog. When I went to Sialkote I found the Queen's Bays had bought a pack of hounds, and they, knowing my enthusiasm for hunting, kindly appointed me as whipper-in, and Major Henry Clerk, the Master, allowed me to help in exercising hounds. I was able to be useful, because I was my own master in the early morning, whereas soldiers in India are often on parade at that time.. So I used to go out exercising with hounds, and took the terriers with me, as this way they learned to run with the pack.

It occurred to me that on drawing some sugar-cane coverts, which are very thick, the terriers would be helpful. Vanity proved to be very useful, She had a gift, which I think some hounds possess, of knowing when there was a "Jack" in the covert. She would trot round at my horse's heels. If she left me and dived into the covert, her sharp little bark soon declared a find. If she did not go in, I knew it was no use. After a week or two the hounds flew to her as to one of themselves. She had an excellent nose and would use it patiently. I have seen her carry the line along the path when not even Sultan, the tender nosed, could own it. It was funny to see this little terrier hunting along, and the big black-and-tan hound in attendance waiting to be sure enough to speak.

It was a very difficult country for a terrier, being intersected with banks and deep muddy ditches, and poor Vanity was left behind when it came to running.

The first season she stuck to the pack somehow, but after that she found it was useless, so when she had enough she would go home, and I never failed on my return to find a little, black, muddy dog curled up in the middle of my bed.

Our hunting-ground was eighteen miles from the cantonments. My servants and horses always went out the night before, and we took up quarters at a dark bungalow and kennels built I believe by the Carabineers when they had the hounds some years before. Vanity never left me as a rule, but she knew when hunting was in prospect, and scrambled up on to the ekka: she understood that there was hard work for her, and always rode all the way. When later, I had a pack of my own, and Vanity was joined by her daughter Vixen, thay gave many proofs of gameness. These two little terriers tackled a wild cat in a covert and killed it before the hounds could come up. On another occasion Vanity pinned a large jackal by the nose, and held on till the pack arrived. We had run the jackal into a covert, and Vanity (of course obliged to skirt) came in after the pack, and met the jackal crawling in the covert. It was a big old dog jackal, and when I brought up the hounds he was trying in vain to shake the terrier off.

On another occasion Vanity actually tackled a good-sized wild boar, and in this conflict she lost an eye. The hounds had brought the boar to bay, and Vanity went in at once and got hold. How she managed to keep hold as long as she did I do not know, but, luckily, when I at last took the hounds away and the boar broke loose from his bay, she was shaken off.

Her daughter Vixen was quite as game, and indeed eventually lost her life by going to ground in a place which she could not be dug out. These were small terriers, not much over twelve pounds, but for strength, gameness, and activity they left nothing to be desired. If I had an occasion to keep working terriers again, I should certainly look out for animals of the type of my old friends, which were handsome too.

Every now and then there is a complaint raised that dog shows are spoiling are terrier. Certainly the type one sees on the bench are not suitable for work. I do not say that would not work no doubt they would; but I think those I have seen are not compact enough, and have not the most effective type of head. If we take the old Scottish breeds in what we may call their primitive state, and compare them with the champions of the modern day show bench, we shall see that the latter have not the type of head which made the former so successful. The old or working type is longer and wider in the head above the eyes, and shorter and stronger in the jaw, than our prize specimens, in which invariably tend toward narrowness and shortness in the head and exaggerated and quite useless in the jaw. In the same way coat, ears, length of body, and many other unimportant points, are bred for, while if one looks in their mouths we see that the teeth most important to a terrier are often inferior. Clean, level, strong teeth are indispensable to a working terrier, but not to a prize winner.

But we may leave the champions at the show bench. They are too valuable to be worked. The risks a terrier takes when he goes into a rocky cavern of the fox or the badger's den are not small. Here and there are terriers bred for work and kept for it. "Points" are not much thought of, but those families are most cherished in which the best qualities are inherited. So that we do in fact, obtain a certain family likeness and quite recognizable. Such, for example, are the Duke of Argyll's Roseneath terriers; the working strain of Poltalloch, with heads almost ideal for work underground; and the Skye, as I have seen him, when untouched by show influence. Active dogs, compact they were, with a reasonable coat, and with suchkeenness and gameness that they were rather difficult to keep aboveground.

So, too, in the South we have the kennel terriers, of which the best known were those of Rev. John Russell, so famous that every terrier of any note at work in the West claims descent from those famous kennels, Or the old type of Badmitton kennel terrier, of which breed the following story is told. A fox once went to ground in a narrow drain; two terriers were running with the pack. The first went in and, unable to get right up to the fox, caught hold of the brush, the only point he could reach. The second terrier also went in, but could not, of course, get far, as his companion blocked the way, so he caught hold of the first terrier's tail. Then came the whipper-in, and he stooped down, put in his arm, and feeling the second terrier he caught hold of him and pulled him out. There was considerable resistance, but at length, to the amusement of the field the second terrier appeared to be holding tight to the tail oh his predecessor, who in turn was holding on to the brush of the fox, which was also drawn in its turn. But the terrier has another softer side. Of all the dogs I have known the terrier has the best memory for friends Even casual friends are not forgotten if once accepted. As for the master, what can exceed the patience and fidelity of the terrier if once his heart is given; and if he is a little jealous and exclusive, after all that is not peculiar to dogs. The terrier is of all dogs the most dependent on human companionship for his efficiency. If your terrier is to do his best for you in the field he must share your home, or if he lives in the kennel you must be often with him; but my experience is that the best for work have been those that have lived with me day and night. A dog so studies your face that he learns to anticipate your wishes, almost to read your expression. Moreover, he picks up a good many words when he is always in the house, and I have generally found there are some words which are so thrilling that they must be spelt out by members of the family. The sound of them is too exciting for the small friends under the table, or seated in their favorite chairs round the room. The terrier, moreover, that lives in the house develops a vocabulary of his own, and one I knew well had three distinct tones. With one he called his mistress when he was in trouble or wanted help; in another, respectfully imperious, he invited a trusted friend to take him out. If however,the servants, with whom he was a great favorite, he would put his head through the banisters of the kitchen staircase and bark sharply and imperiously for one of them to come. Each tone was known and recognized, and I never knew him to deceive by using one in place of the others.

Printed in the United Kingdom
by Lightning Source UK Ltd.
124437UK00001B/344/A